RAIN POWER

A Young Professional's Guide to Achieving Wealth and Happiness

The powerful six-step plan that teaches young lawyers, accountants, investment bankers, consultants, and other service providers how to reach their professional and personal goals by becoming rainmakers.

STEVEN ZUCKERMAN, ESQ.

ISBN: 978-0692281635

Contents

About the Author

Steve Zuckerman is a Managing Director of Farlie Turner & Co., a prominent investment bank that provides merger and acquisition, private placement, and financial advisory services to middle market companies.

In 2006, Steve launched Farlie Turner's Special Situations Group and has built it into a nationally recognized and market-leading practice. Steve was named as one of the Top 40 Dealmakers Under 40 Years Old in the United States in 2013 and was recognized the following year as one of the Top 100 Restructuring and Turnaround Professionals. Steve has originated and led several transactions that have received various national awards, including Special Situations Deal of the Year.

Early in his career, he practiced law with the nationally recognized law firm of Berger Singerman, where he specialized in restructuring financially distressed companies. During his tenure as an attorney, Steve was twice recognized as an "Up and Comer," an honor reserved for fewer than two percent of Florida attorneys under forty years old.

Steve is also the co-founder of a venture-backed health-care technology company. In addition, he founded Leaders of Tomorrow, an exclusive networking and mentoring organization comprised of South Florida's next generation of business and community leaders.

He earned a B.A. from Boston University and a J.D. from the University of Miami School of Law, both with honors, and also holds a Series 79 license. Steve serves as a subject matter expert for the innovative LawWithoutWalls Program at the University of Miami School of Law and has lectured on the topics of professional development and "How to Analyze, Value, and Acquire a Business."

Steve lives in Miami Beach with his wife and two daughters.

Preface

I've spent the majority of my career in professional services, initially as an attorney and in the last seven years as an investment banker. As a result, I'm writing from a place of experience. I understand the challenges and confusion associated with being a young professional. By imparting the six-step blueprint in this book, I hope to greatly enhance your journey on the rocky road of professional services. This methodology, which I developed and honed over the last fifteen years, enabled me to start a new division for a prominent investment bank in my early thirties and successfully build that division into a market-leading position. Over the last five years, I've generated over $10 million in revenue and have originated numerous successful M&A transactions. I am reluctant to admit this because it sounds arrogant, but it's important for you to know that these strategies work. These strategies will also have the unintended consequence of improving many other aspects of your life.

If I can do it, so can you. Some people think you need to have a certain set of educational, familial, and financial credentials to achieve success in the hyper-competitive professional services industry. This negative thinking can become a powerful self-fulfilling prophecy. In my own personal experience, this is simply not true. My pedigree is not stereotypical of what you would expect from a successful investment banker and attorney.

I grew up in a small apartment in a subsidized housing complex in Queens, New York, flanked by public housing projects. I did not have family connections; my mom was a homemaker (a fabulous one at that), and my stepfather owned a small hardware store in Brooklyn.

I am not a natural born leader fraught with fortitude, but I cultivated inner strength as a result of my surroundings. I was not born with the gift of gab; in fact, I was shy and have had to work hard to become more extroverted. Unlike many of my colleagues, I did not attend Ivy League academic institutions, nor am I usually the person with the highest IQ in the room. But I am filled with desire, ambition, determination, and persistence, and I suspect that you are, too; otherwise, you would not be reading this book. I am also highly mindful about how I interact with and treat others, which I believe is the recipe for success.

Thank you for reading this book. I hope my labors help you avoid the pitfalls of professional services and achieve wealth and happiness beyond your dreams.

Introduction

This book is about your favorite subject, you. More specifically, your future.

No, I'm not your mom or dad giving you a lecture. I'm a professional just like you who made some choices—both good and bad—and I'm passing along my experiences. The first thing you should know as you embark on your professional career is that you have a choice between two paths. One is average; the other is exceptional. If you want average, then please pass this book on to someone else. You don't need my advice on how to be average. But if you want to have an exceptional career in professional services—one as a lawyer, accountant, investment banker, consultant, or the like—then this book is for you.

By exceptional, I mean both achieving the financial wealth you desire and finding a deep feeling of happiness and satisfaction that goes far beyond the number of zeros in your bank account. I want you to have both—financial success and personal fulfillment. And the key to creating an exceptional professional services career can be summed up in three words: Be a rainmaker.

No, it has nothing to do with the weather or agriculture.

In the business world, a rainmaker is a person who

secures new clients and additional business opportunities for his or her firm. A rainmaker generates substantial new business by connecting with new clients and by prompting current clients to pursue additional projects. A rainmaker is the lifeblood of the organization upon whom the organization depends for its survival, stability, and growth. As a result, a rainmaker—a client and revenue generator—is the most valuable currency in the professional services industry.

Being a rainmaker will dramatically improve your professional and personal life because it buys you freedom. Freedom to focus on projects and tasks that interest you, freedom to earn considerably more money, freedom to spend more time with your family and friends, and freedom to pursue other interests. Why? Because all of a firm's expenses—including the generous salaries and bonuses enjoyed by its professionals—are paid by clients. Clients are delivered by rainmakers. Rainmakers fuel the engine of the professional services industry; without them, there would be a lot of smart people standing around with nothing to do.

Young professionals are too often shielded from this harsh reality. They join firms, are spoon-fed work, and pay little attention to the fuel that drives the growth and success of their firms' engines—business development. This is a mistake that has profound implications. Ignoring business development at the early stages of a professional career seems like a nice reprieve, but it is the path of increasing resistance, frustration, and stress, as well as considerably less professional and personal satisfaction. It is a mistake that I hope to help you, the young professional, avoid. You can embark on the path to an exceptional career through my practical, six-step program that will transform you into a rainmaker.

Money is important, but there is an even bigger goal at stake: personal satisfaction and happiness. While being a rainmaker is the currency of the professional services industry, being happy is the ultimate currency of life. By transforming yourself into a rainmaker in accordance with the principles articulated in this book, you'll be empowered to build a bridge to a life beyond your dreams.

The strategies outlined here are simple and practical. This is a program of action, not theories, written from the perspective of experience, not an ivory tower. This is not a get rich quick scheme but a formula to achieve not only a more lucrative career but an exponentially more enjoyable life. If you consistently follow this blueprint, you will enrich your life with greater wealth, meaning, and happiness.

Let's get started!

CHAPTER ONE

Two Career Paths

Every young person starts his or her professional service career with high expectations. From professors, parents, and colleagues, we hear lines like, "You will be wealthy and have the opportunity to experience the best life has to offer. Your career will be meaningful. You will be happy and fulfilled." In reality, these beliefs are illusions and false hopes. They remind me of a great line from the movie, *The Usual Suspects*: "The greatest trick the Devil ever pulled was convincing the world he didn't exist." As smart, determined overachievers, we diligently pursue personal and professional happiness by achieving success as lawyers, accountants, consultants, investment bankers, investment advisors, etc. We believe with every fiber of our being that hard work and technical proficiency will enable us to earn a lot of money and reap the benefits associated with achieving wealth—power, prestige, freedom, financial security, and eternal happiness. We are so invested in the notion that hard work and sacrifice will be handsomely rewarded that we are unwilling to question or explore the veracity of our preconceived notions. Strangely, our parents and professors also fail to enlighten us, either as a result of their lack of knowledge or their unwillingness to deter us.

The reality is that being a skilled and hardworking professional service provider is simply the price of admission. It does not guarantee wealth, job security, personal freedom, or happiness. Have you ever noticed colleagues within your firm or profession who seem to have it all yet appear unhappy, irritable, and discontented? Sadly, the pot of gold at the end of the rainbow—that reward for all your hard work, sacrifice, and dedication—is an illusion.

Unfortunately, many young professionals wake up to this reality after the golden handcuffs are firmly secured. I hope to save you this fate by arming you with the knowledge and tools to change your beliefs and the trajectory of your career. The road to professional and personal prosperity is contingent upon molding your behavior, attitude, and overall career strategy such that you are transformed into a rainmaker.

The Average Career Path

PROFESSIONAL SERVICE PROVIDERS TEND to follow the same long and arduous path. Let's look at a typical young professional whom we'll call John.

John worked hard in school, incurring debt and making personal sacrifices along the way. As he anxiously awaited the wealth and prestige of becoming a professional, notions that years of sacrifice and hard work would pay off permeated his thinking. Then, after many years of school, it finally happened. The job offers started flowing, and things seemed to be going according to his master plan.

As John commenced his professional career, he felt that his goals were within reach. He soon had an office in an impressive skyscraper, an administrative assistant, and an endless supply of fancy business cards. He regularly ate at good restaurants, bought designer clothes, and stayed at nice hotels. Financial independence felt nice. His family and friends were proud and bragged about his accomplishments and even started calling for advice. All was well...for a while.

The honeymoon phase abruptly ended, and John realized that being a professional was really challenging and entailed an extraordinary commitment to his office chair. The work was often tedious and mundane and certainly fell short of the intellectually stimulating work that was alluded to during the lavish recruitment outings. Should he have been surprised? After all, did he really expect to start off doing glamorous courtroom work, negotiating multi-million dollar deals, or overhauling a company's business strategy? Researching case law, drafting offering memorandums, reviewing general ledgers, reading tedious research reports, putting together pitch books, and performing other mind-numbing tasks until all hours of the night comprised John's life. Making matters exponentially worse, there was an asshole in his chain of command who appeared to be singularly focused on ruining John's nights and weekends, purely as payback to the asshole who had done the same thing to *him* 20 years earlier.

John comforted himself by thinking this was normal;

it was like pledging a fraternity. He could tough it out for a few years until he achieved a little more seniority, and then things would get better. But years went by, and he realized that not much had changed, except the bags under his eyes had grown darker, and his lower back ached from sitting all day. He was still working over 60 hours each week and had slowly realized that being a professional is akin to being a poorly compensated skilled laborer. After he figured out what it equaled on an hourly basis, the low-six figure salary didn't seem so rewarding—especially when taking into account his lower back pain and unhealthy pale skin caused by his underexposure to natural sunlight. He start resenting, or perhaps envying, the slacker from high school who was now a plumber and was "taking home" $100 per hour. John was lucky if he got two weeks off a year, half of which were spent on his smartphone and at the windowless office center of some Ritz Carlton hotel.

Suddenly, the enigmatic voicemails he received became more interesting: "Hi, this is Jane Smith," one said. "Please call me back as soon as possible. I need to speak with you regarding an important matter." No company name, no description of the "important matter." Obviously, a recruiter. So, he took what I call the "more-and-better bait" that things would be better, more fun, more challenging, and more lucrative at the *Pieh Skie* firm, since they claimed to value firm culture and work–life balance. After all, it said so on their website under the tab entitled "firm culture."

John eagerly joined the *Pieh Skie* firm, reveled in his $25,000 raise, and enjoyed another honeymoon period during which he thought things might actually be different. However, a year went by, and he arrived at the unfortunate but inevitable conclusion that everything was the same—except, of course, for the identity of the new and somehow bigger asshole in his chain of command. It turned out that the "quality of life" and "work–life balance" section of the firm's web site were developed by an outside advertising firm, and that the senior partners never got the memo.

He was now at a crossroad. Six long years had gone by, and he wondered whether he had chosen the right profession. He thought about his options, and realized he did not have many practical ones. Teaching or not-for-profit work were possibilities, but with BMW payments and appearances to keep up, John needed that six-figure salary.

He talked to his parents and friends about buying a Subway franchise, gas station, and ten other unrealistic ideas and continued to get the same reassuring advice that everything would be better once he became a partner or managing director—the holy grails of professional services. He explained that being a professional was all-consuming, and that most professionals never make enough money or achieve enough seniority to emerge from the rat race. The taskmasters at work were ever-changing and impossible to please since they each had a different style, temperament, and work schedule. The only way to appease his demanding superiors, albeit temporarily, was to be incredibly responsive, which was a euphemism for "work all the time."

That's when Dad interrupted the pity party and

provided some good paternal advice. "Son, I know it's been hard, but if it were easy, anyone could do it. Once you become a partner, you will have your own team of youngsters doing all the grunt work. Plus, you'll make a lot more money."

Maybe Dad was right—becoming a partner or managing director was the answer. Once again, John refocused his efforts on becoming a partner or MD and looked forward to the days of free time, less work, and a lot more money. A few years later, he finally arrived and became a partner! His parents, friends, and family were even more proud. The title came with a bigger office with a view, a car allowance, a life insurance policy, and better health insurance. He had some twenty-year-olds to do his work, and that part was great, but he still wasn't working less; he still had no real input in his firm's strategic decisions, and his compensation hadn't significantly increased. It was a sad revelation: being a partner or managing director didn't mean he was a "real" partner. It just meant more bureaucracy and a title that was more impressive to outsiders. When he inquired about becoming a true equity partner, they told him that he did not qualify because he had not generated sufficient revenue. No one ever emphasized or articulated this criterion before, so he felt like he'd been duped.

John hastily called his favorite recruiter, only to realize that his managing partner had not gone mad, and he finally learned the truth. He was simply not marketable without his own clients, otherwise known as a portable book of business. In fact, as a high paid "working partner," he was perhaps one of the most vulnerable professionals in his firm. The pot at the end of the rainbow was empty. What happened? What went wrong? Did he really just spend the last ten years and twenty thousand hours of his life making sacrifices only to achieve a Pyrrhic victory?

Suddenly, it occurred to him—he was in golden handcuffs and dependent on a low six-figure income. He had achieved a modicum of professional success, but not his dream of financial independence, freedom, and flexibility. He mistakenly assumed that if he worked hard, consistently delivered a quality work product, and was a good corporate citizen respected by his colleagues, he would achieve greater independence and financial freedom.

Now, don't feel bad for John; this is a common misperception that can be avoided. Adding insult to injury was the fact that he had no one to blame but himself. His firm did not forbid him from becoming a rainmaker. They simply did not require it at the outset of his career because he was being hired to be a worker, grinder, and doer—not a business generator.

Understand Your Value Proposition

LIKE JOHN, IF YOU are not a standalone revenue generator, the moment your firm loses a few big clients, or the economy tanks, you become a *cost item*. Unless you are truly gifted with a unique skill set—and let's face it, most of us are not—you are dispensable and serve at the pleasure of the "real partners" (i.e., owners) of your firm as long as *they* generate enough work for you to do.

If this sounds like hyperbole, consider the failings of

some of the largest and most prominent professional service providers over the last decade—Arthur Andersen; BearingPoint (previously KPMG Consulting); Dewey & LeBoeuf; Brobeck, Phleger & Harrison; and many others. Imagine being used to a comfortable six-figure salary when your firm suddenly downsizes or collapses. You have nowhere to go because other firms are experiencing the same issues that impacted your firm, and the market is flooded with smart and talented professionals. Think about the financial collapse around 2007–2009. There were not too many firms hiring real estate lawyers focused on development. Do you want to beg people for a job after you busted your ass for years at your prior firm and before that at college and graduate school ? Do you want to deplete your savings or, even worse, borrow money from a family member or friend? If you prefer to never experience such humiliation, want to have options and control over your professional destiny, then I encourage you to continue reading.

There is a seismic disconnect between theory and practice, and between the classroom and the courtroom. To put it more bluntly, in the absence of relevant work experience, you don't have many practical skills after you graduate from college or a higher-level graduate program. Compounding matters, you don't know what you don't know. Accordingly, a lot of money is spent on training and educating young professionals. Clients do not like subsidizing the mistakes of young professionals, so there are inevitable write-offs of your time due to your lack of experience.

Your value proposition will begin to shift after a few

years. Once you develop a basic understanding of your chosen profession, and you can handle matters with minimal supervision, efficiently respond to client inquiries, and manage the workflow of more junior professionals, you become extremely valuable and marketable. As opposed to being a burden to your more senior colleagues, you are now of tremendous value, and the value you are generating significantly exceeds your compensation.

Soon, the glory years will fade. Without your own clients or a book of business, your value begins to level out and even decline as your seniority increases. That's not to say an experienced and skilled practitioner is not valuable; he or she is very valuable. However, if the work dries up when market conditions inevitably change, you will be one of the first to go because you are set in your ways and require a larger salary, which can make you a significant burden. You will also have limited marketability to other firms, who are likely experiencing the same challenges.

Without clients to service, your intellect and skills are of no consequence to your firm. You are a cost item, and you are dispensable. Even at a busy firm with lots of clients, a skilled laborer is generally replaceable. It may cause some minor client service issues but usually no permanent damage.

The Rainmaker Career Path

IF YOU'RE FEELING DEPRESSED and deceived by your career choice, I want to let you know that your career trajectory need not follow the typical pattern. There is an important exception to the tedium, grueling work, and modest wages of the "average" professional services career path. The exception comes from generating significant revenue and profits for your firm, which means transforming yourself into a rainmaker.

This is very important: rainmakers are the exception, not the rule. Unlike "service partners" who are dispensable, rainmakers are *indispensable* because *they drive profitability and growth*. Once you establish yourself as a rainmaker, your position changes quickly and dramatically. One significant benefit is the ability to earn a lot more money. On the average career path, the formula that is used for compensating most professionals is fairly simple and results in a glass ceiling. It centers on the professional's hourly rate and number of hours worked per year. Neither of these variables is elastic. There is a limit to how much clients are willing to pay per hour for a professional's time, which since the Great Recession has started to plateau. At the same time, there is a limit to the number of hours any human being can work.

This compensation model is not leverageable. After taking into account office overhead, other non-billable staff, write-offs, marketing, and other expenses, professionals are typically paid (in my experience) approximately twenty to forty percent of their billable revenue. The chart on the next page reflects the relatively inelastic compensation range for a professional based on varying hourly rates and billable hours (it assumes that the professional is paid thirty percent of his or her billable revenue, and no billable time is written off):

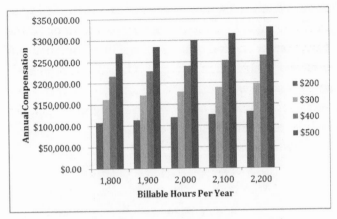

As a rainmaker, your base compensation may be on par with your colleagues, but it will be dramatically enhanced based on the amount of revenue you generate from your clients. This can result in additional compensation of hundreds of thousands of dollars more per year at a relatively young age and additional millions over the course of your career.

Earning considerably more money is a significant benefit, but by no means is it the only reason for becoming a rainmaker. Other advantages include the ability to delegate work to your colleagues (younger and older), increased flexibility and working fewer traditional in-office hours, participating in work-related events that do not seem like work (i.e., charity events, golf tournaments, dinners, trips, conferences), greater independence and less micromanagement, and the ability to focus on the fun parts of your job, not the inane ones.

As a rainmaker with a book of business, you are indispensable. Whether with your current firm, another one, or your own, you always have options and the ability to earn a significant income. If your firm collapses or downsizes, your phone will be ringing with offers, and you will control your professional destiny. You will have more time for family, travel, community service, hobbies, and whatever else fulfills you. After all, work is a means to these ends, and not the other way around.

Anyone Can Become a Rainmaker

BEFORE WE DELVE INTO the details, it is important to dispel some preconceived notions regarding the skills or qualities a successful rainmaker must possess. You need to be smart and have a command of your chosen profession, but you need not be recognized as the leading industry expert in the country. Being able to communicate well and connect with people is necessary, but you don't have to be a natural extrovert. You must be focused on client service, but you need not, nor should you, be billing the most hours.

And to dispel one of the biggest myths—being a rainmaker does not require you to manipulate situations, so as to engender a positive outcome only for yourself. In fact, the opposite is true. As you will appreciate by the end of this book, the only way to become a successful rainmaker is to truly care about and help others solve their problems and succeed in their endeavors. The concept of giving more than you take is woven through every fiber of this book because it is the common thread that engenders improvement in all facets of your life, not just your career.

CHAPTER 2

The Six-Step Rainmaker Development Plan

Attorneys, accountants, auditors, investment bankers, consultants, and other service providers all deliver a variation of the same service segment: professional advice. Clients and referral sources have many options. The world is full of smart, capable, and hardworking service providers who are ready and willing to work long hours and offer good advice. In the United States, there are approximately:

> - 1.2 million attorneys
> - 1.3 million accounting, finance and audit professionals
> - 700,000 management consultants*

The good news is that despite the abundance of smart service providers, you need not resign yourself to being a commodity. You can easily distinguish yourself in the crowded space by consistently adding value to your client services with the goal of becoming a trusted advisor.

People do business with professionals they like, trust, and respect. It is within your power to control these

---

* American Bar Association and U.S. Department of Labor

perceptions. The way your clients and referral sources perceive you starts with your personal brand, and, as we know from the multi-billion dollar advertising industry, brands can be shaped. But before delving into personal brand building and the other steps, it is important to establish your goals.

I have broken down the elements of a highly effective, long-term business development strategy into six steps, the first of which is goal setting. Follow these steps in order, but keep in mind that steps overlap and require consistent effort, refinement, and improvement. This plan is not static and should evolve as time goes on.

The Six-Step Business Development Plan

Set Goals   Build Brand   Accelerate Growth   Define & Build Network   Work Your Network   Find a Mentor

Step 1 - Set Goals

Much like an architect would not start building a house without a rendering of what he or she intends to build, you should not set out to become a rainmaker without establishing specific goals. This will serve as your roadmap. Studies have shown that people with similar backgrounds and educations are much more likely to succeed if they have specific goals documented in writing. As Napoleon Hill said, "Whatever the mind can conceive and believe, it can achieve." Goals are the bridges between dreams and reality. They motivate and remind you of the desired result and help you measure success. Sometimes goal-setting can be complex; in this instance, it is fairly simple because the byproduct of business development is easily quantifiable.

As a rainmaker, your goal is to generate revenue, which is an easy metric to track. Your goals should be aspirational and ambitious, yet not so aggressive as to render them unachievable. For example, if you originated less than $50,000 in revenue in the last calendar year, I suggest you aim for $100,000–$150,000 in the first full year after implementing the strategies outlined in this book; set a goal of $250,000–$500,000 the second year and $1,000,000 in the third year. Think about doubling your goal each year until you are consistently generating several million dollars per year.

In addition to generating revenue, you should focus on constantly adding new clients. You want to avoid building a practice around only a handful of clients because losing one can have a major impact on your financial performance. In the parlance of mergers & acquisitions (M&A), this is referred to as customer concentration. Customer concentration is such a fundamental issue that most private equity firms will apply a significant discount to a profitable business that generates most of its revenue from a handful of clients, especially if the product or service that is being sold can easily be acquired elsewhere.

That said, the *quality* of new clients is significantly more important than the *quantity*. You will find that low-revenue clients can drain your time and energy. The key is to have a good mix of high quality, recurring clients and referral sources. Once you have developed an annual revenue goal, I recommend two simple strategies to increase your likelihood of achieving it.

First, tell other people, such as your supervising partner or significant other. Write down your goal. Consider embarking on this business development journey with a colleague at work or a friend at another firm and create joint goals. These tactics are designed to create accountability and a heightened level of commitment.

Second, think about your goal daily and visualize yourself achieving it. Close your eyes and think about sitting in your annual review and proudly recounting how you achieved your goal and generated meaningful revenue for your firm. Think about the satisfaction you will feel by achieving your goals and how your bonus will reward your rainmaking success. Now, think about how you are going to spend the extra income—perhaps going on a great trip, making a significant donation, buying a house, or throwing a party for a loved one. Visualization is a powerful technique, frequently used by professional athletes, that assists the brain with subconsciously developing strategies and behaviors to accomplish a goal.

In addition to setting revenue and new client goals, there is another, even more critical, goal you must establish and consistently achieve. As you will hear throughout this book, if you do not help other people succeed, you will not maximize your success at work or life. Accordingly, it is critical to establish a referral revenue goal to reflect the amount of revenue you are going to refer to your *target referral sources*, which is discussed in detail in subsequent chapters. For now, simply make a mental note that an essential component of your business development strategy will be consistently referring business to your target referral sources. This amount should equate to, at a minimum, your own revenue goal, and should ideally be 25% more than your personal goal. For example, if your revenue goal is $500,000 in a given year, your target referral source revenue goal should be $625,000. If you are not giving more than you are taking, your chances for long-term success in business (and life) are greatly diminished.

Happiness – The Ultimate Goal

This book will help you amass wealth, influence, and prestige. Enjoy them; I do. I love the freedom, luxuries, and ease that money helps me obtain. But I've come to appreciate the fact that accumulating money, power, and prestige is not the basis of a happy and successful life; it is only one component.

I finally realized that material wealth alone could never make me truly happy. If material wealth was the *end* as opposed to the *means*, I determined that I could never get enough of it to satisfy my desires. Wealth and prestige are moving targets. This epiphany led me to consider new definitions of success not measured exclusively by the zeros in my bank account, such as:

> *To laugh often and much; to win the respect of intelligent people and the affection of children; to earn the appreciation of honest critics and to endure the betrayal of false friends; to appreciate beauty; to find the best in others; to leave the world a bit better whether by a healthy child, a garden patch or a redeemed social*

*condition; to know even one life has breathed easier
because you have lived. This is to have succeeded.*

                                        – Ralph Waldo Emerson

*To me, success is the ongoing process of striving to
become more. It is the opportunity to grow emotionally, socially, spiritually, physiologically, intellectually,
and financially while contributing in some positive
way to others. The road to success is always under
construction. It is a progressive course, not an end to
be reached.*

                                              – Tony Robbins

Without getting on my spiritual high-horse, I simply
encourage you to explore your purpose in life and to get
in touch with your true self. The path of self-discovery is
amazingly enlightening and will help you put your career
into perspective. It will also help you develop non-career,
life goals to engender happiness.

Being a professional service provider is hard. It is hyper-competitive, arduous, and stressful. It often requires
an adversarial nature to advance your and your clients' interests. This can take a significant toll over time and make
you a jaded, cynical, and unhappy person. The halls of
gleaming office towers and marble-laden offices throughout the world are filled with well-paid yet irritable, dis-
satisfied, and cantankerous professional souls. As you set
your specific financial goals, which is an important first
step of the rainmaking process, I encourage you to not
lose sight of the ultimate goal—a meaningful and happy
life. Because it's predicated on helping others succeed,
becoming a rainmaker in accordance with the principles

outlined in this book is the bridge to a more fulfilling, meaningful, and joyous life. I have found that the more connected and helpful I am to others, the more pleasure and meaning I experience. I am confident you will, too.

Step 2 - Build Your Brand

In the professional services arena, clients are looking for someone they can trust to handle their problems, resolve complex challenges, or take advantage of an opportunity. In doing so, professionals are acting on behalf of their clients and serving as an extension of their persona and brand.

Take an honest look at how you present yourself and ask others how they see you. If you appear stressed, anxious, egotistical, or overly aggressive, it may not be the perception clients want reflected upon them. If you dress sloppily or appear unhealthy, what does that say about your confidence and self-esteem? Can clients trust you with confidential information if you share non-public information about other clients? What does it say about your judgment and discretion if you have posted inappropriate comments or pictures on Facebook, Twitter, or Instagram? If the answers to these hypothetical questions are not obvious, please stop reading this book—it cannot help you.

It is critical to remember that all of your actions and choices, from how you speak and interact with others, to your personal style and office appearance, form an unconscious impression in the minds of your potential clients and referral sources. Because perception drives reality, you always want to make sure that you and your actions convey trust, professionalism, genuine interest, discretion, confidence, honesty, sincerity, and success. You must avoid being perceived as dishonest, detached, stressed, distracted, egotistical, rude, insincere, or disorganized. There are simple ways to do this and enhance your personal brand:

1. **Look the part.** Dress neatly and professionally. Keep your office, desk, and car clean.

2. **Be responsive.** It is imperative to be incredibly responsive to emails and voicemails. I try to return emails and calls within a few hours. If you are going to be unavailable for most of the day (or longer) and unable to access your email or voicemail, change your outbound voicemail to reflect that, and do the same with an "out-of-office" email. Train your administrative support to respond to your emails and voicemails and to direct clients/referral sources to a pre-designated colleague who has been prepared to address the issue.

3. **Control your tone.** Manage the sound and tone of your voice to sound confident, positive, and engaging. At the same time, avoid appearing stressed, rushed, or distracted.

4. **Do not multi-task.** It's often obvious to the person with whom you are interacting, and it connotes a lack of interest and respect. Further, despite what you may think, it's actually counter-productive to

try and accomplish several things at once, as none are being done well.

5. **Demonstrate sound judgment.** Do not permit a lapse of judgment in your personal and professional life. If you have radical or prejudicial beliefs or unusual personal interests, keep them to yourself. Do not tweet about them or post them on Facebook.

6. **Be prepared.** Never walk into a meeting with potential clients or referral sources without Googling them to uncover relevant information and reviewing their website, social media, and professional background in detail. Research industry trends and current events, understand their business, read recent news stories involving their industry, gather some ideas as to how you can help them, and develop some insightful questions. As Winston Churchill noted, "Preparation is—if not the key to genius—then at least the key to sounding like a genius." Try and find a way to weave your preparation into your discussion. For example, "I was reviewing your recent press releases on your company's aggressive expansion into the West Coast market, as well as the article that was published in the *Herald* a few months ago, and was wondering how this expansion effort has impacted your performance, given the sudden increase in freight costs?"

7. **Be proactive.** Send prospective clients and referral sources information, news stories, and resources that are helpful to their business; however,

never inundate them with irrelevant or self-serving information.

8. **Communicate effectively.** Being articulate conveys intelligence and confidence. Avoid using colloquialisms and pay attention to speech patterns and fillers such as "you know," "like," "whatever," or even "um" or "ah." They make you appear less intelligent and are a distraction and irritant to the person with whom you are communicating. If you have these speech patterns, be aware when you are speaking and practice removing them.

9. **Treat everyone equally.** It is important to treat administrative assistants, receptionists, wait-staff, door attendants, and any other person you encounter on a daily basis with the same level of respect and courtesy that you would bestow upon a CEO or senior partner. Not only do they have more influence on your professional career than you think, it is simply the right thing to do.

10. **Be authentic, humble, and honest.** You can be the smartest, hardest working, most experienced professional in the world, but if you are arrogant or inauthentic, you will not connect with others. More importantly, your honesty and integrity must be beyond reproach. Honesty is absolutely essential to building trust and respect. It is the foundation for all professional relationships. Do not exaggerate or mislead. If you make a mistake, own up to it quickly.

Some of these principles may seem obvious and rudimentary, but many professionals fail to consistently incorporate them in all of their affairs. A positive personal brand evokes trust and confidence and is a critical attribute of a successful rainmaker. Incorporating these principles in your daily life is a quick and easy way to gain a competitive advantage.

What's Your Value Proposition?

There are many smart lawyers, consultants, accountants, and other professionals; however, very few professionals originate new business because they are the smartest or the best. Technical mastery is expected; it's the entry fee to the world of being a professional service provider and getting paid six figures at a young age. If professionals relied solely on their intelligence and work ethic to generate revenue, the halls of professional service firms across the country would be deserted. In other words, when you are marketing to a perspective client or referral source, how do you differentiate yourself from the thousands of other capable professionals?

Regurgitating where you went to college or graduate school is not the right answer. You need to be able to convey your *value proposition* in a way that demonstrates why you are special and why someone should spend the time getting to know you. Let's start off with answering the question, "What do you do?" It is important to have a brief description of what solutions you deliver (not what you are) and what differentiates you and your firm. If you're asked this question, and you respond by saying, "I am an attorney," you have provided little useful information and squandered an opportunity to make an impression or have a continued dialogue. If, however, you say, "I'm an employment litigation attorney focused on helping corporations mitigate frivolous litigation by employees," you've described exactly what you do and how you can add value in a succinct manner.

Many professionals make the mistake of treating the "what do you do" question as an invitation to provide a diatribe on their credentials. They start dropping names of Ivy League schools, people they know, and awards they've won. Building credibility is important, but always keep in mind that your clients and referral sources are more interested in themselves and their problems than you—especially when you first meet.

While you should have a rehearsed positioning statement, it is important to be flexible in order to accommodate your audience's background, needs, or wants. If it is an impromptu meeting, I always ask penetrating questions, so that I can mold my positioning accordingly. If I am planning for a meeting, I modify my positioning statement to appeal to the person with whom I am meeting.

For example, a few years ago I pitched a client who was also interviewing an investment bank with relevant industry specialization. I learned that the CEO was leaning toward hiring the other investment bank because of their industry expertise. Because our firm is industry agnostic, it would have been foolish to walk into the pitch meeting emphasizing this point, even though I think broad experience is more advantageous. Instead, I thought about how to position my experience to appeal to his desire to hire someone with relevant industry expertise. I walked into our meeting and proactively stated that I thought it was important to hire an industry expert. He nodded his head in complete agreement and then asked me how many restaurant chains I had sold.

I explained that once a company enters the zone of insolvency, "distress" becomes its primary industry. It does not matter whether you sell hamburgers, repair airplanes, build hot tubs, or retail golf equipment—all industries in which I have done deals. What you make or sell is not nearly as important as hiring an investment bank with experience navigating the choppy waters of financial distress with a successful track record of helping companies raise capital to ensure survival. That resonated with the client, and our firm was hired.

Always remember that clients hire professionals to solve their problems or capitalize on an opportunity. Be sure to structure your value proposition in terms of how you are going to help them accomplish what they need or want.

Be Likeable

A GREAT RAINMAKER IS often a chameleon and has the ability to modify his or her style based on the needs, desires, personality, motivations, and experiences of others. Being likeable and establishing rapport is one of the most important aspects influencing someone's decision to hire or refer you to a potential client. A client may perceive you as a great strategy consultant with a lot of relevant experience, but if he or she does not like you as a person, you may not obtain business opportunities with that client.

Unlike trust and respect, which are earned over time through multiple interactions, being perceived as likeable or unlikeable usually occurs in mere moments. Most successful politicians, actors, and rainmakers have the "likeability" factor. If you are not likeable, you will not get the opportunity to build a relationship and develop the trust and respect that evolves over time. Everyone can make a calculated effort to become more likeable regardless of his or her personality. You do not need to undergo a complete personality transformation; you simply need to focus on developing "likeability" as a skill in the same way as you would focus on building muscle in the gym.

Dale Carnegie, in his renowned book, *How to Win Friends and Influence People*, discusses many strategies for being likeable, couched in the euphemism "how to win friends." I recommend reading the entire book. One of his most insightful observations is that people have a deep desire to feel important and appreciated and that showing genuine interest and appreciation for people will result in friendships that are more meaningful. It is essential to be a great listener, to encourage people to talk about themselves, and to speak in terms of the other person's interests. He famously remarked, "You can make more friends in two months by becoming really interested in other people than you can in two years by trying to get other people interested in you."

In a nutshell, you can dramatically improve your likeability factor by simply acknowledging these fundamental aspects of human nature and sacrificing your own needs to feel important and be the center of attention. Why should you do this? It's simple: people do business with people they like. Buying professional services is an emotional experience in which trust and likeability often trump logic and reason. Improve your ability to generate business by consistently employing the following "likeability" strategies in your daily interactions with people:

1. When conversing with people, listen twice as much as you speak, especially when you first meet someone. Listening does not mean simply nodding your head and waiting for your turn to talk. It means carefully and empathetically paying attention to what is being said, the tone and body language with which the ideas are being communicated, and assessing how the speaker is affected. Being an excellent listener is especially important in the context of professional services, where our job is to deliver solutions to a client's problems. Actively listening enables you to carefully define a problem, which is the most important aspect when developing an appropriate solution. To be truly effective, we must also pick up on verbal and non-verbal cues, so that our advice is appropriately packaged to maximize its impact.

2. Ask a lot of questions to uncover common ground, interests, and passions. People gravitate toward

people they perceive as similar, who share the same interests, experiences, and values. Ask open-ended and follow-up questions, but interject statements to avoid making your discussion seem like an interrogation.

3. Smile and exude a positive mental attitude. It's Psychology 101. People generally prefer to be happy than sad, and since we sense each other's mood and energy, people are more attracted toward those giving off positive energy. Avoid being negative, complaining, or judging others at all costs.

4. Do not be a know-it-all (even if you are right) or a "one-upper" (someone who always attempts to outdo the experience described in the last person's remark). Instead, listen intently and be open to new ideas. Do not be afraid to show your vulnerability by admitting that you do not know something. Be humble and gracious and make the other person feel important.

5. Be interesting. You should read one or more newspapers each day (especially the business section), business magazines, and relevant publications. Based on the background and interests of the person with whom you are meeting, interject comments regarding relevant current events, sports, and music. Tell a funny story about your kids or parents. Stay away from politics or religion unless you know for certain you share the same views as the person with whom you are speaking.

6. Because non-verbal cues play an important role in communication, pay attention to body language. Show enthusiasm in your voice and body language and maintain steady eye contact. Avoid body language that implies that you are closed off, such as crossing your arms across your chest, and never email or text in the middle of a discussion. Focusing completely on the person with whom you are speaking makes a strong impression.

7. Always introduce yourself and remember people's names. A trick I use to remember names of people I meet is to envision writing it on their forehead with an imaginary pen or immediately repeating it after being introduced – "It's nice meeting you Andrew."

8. Be yourself. Too many people act in a way they think they should, which results in mundane, superficial conversations. Showing some vulnerability, being authentic, and demonstrating empathy are the quickest ways to build a bond.

9. Consciously diffuse your internal programming (i.e., "look at me, listen to me"). Strive to understand people rather than hoping they understand you.

10. Exude confidence and passion. People are naturally drawn towards self-confidence, especially if it is authentic and humble, as well as energetic, enthusiastic, and passionate.

All of these strategies revolve around turning yourself outward and focusing on the needs and interests of other people and empathizing with their feelings. According to the Oxford Dictionaries, "I" is one of the most frequently used words in the English language. Prolific rainmakers more frequently use the word "you" as it captures the essence of humanity. You must become adept at adjusting your behavior based on your prospect's needs and personality. Of course, this must be done with sincere and genuine interest. You cannot fake it. If you seek to understand people and help them succeed, you will be amazed at how they will do the same for you. These techniques not only make you more likeable, but also help you create deeper and more genuine connections with others, which will enrich your life.

Promoting Your Brand

IT IS IMPORTANT TO be hardworking, skillful, and well informed, but your success will be limited if these traits are not widely recognized by clients and referral sources. Writing articles and speaking at conferences is a good way to demonstrate your expertise to a large audience and build credibility. Being quoted in the news or relevant publications also helps. When a credible publication relies on your expertise, it positions you as an expert and immediately boosts your brand.

Identify trade journals, newspapers, relevant web publications, and business reporters. Learn about stories they cover, and then pitch them as an available resource or on a particular idea. Most journalists provide their email addresses after their stories. Send them an email commenting on a piece they wrote—everyone likes praise. Let them know your expertise and that you are interested in being a source of insightful commentary. You may be surprised to learn that journalists get many of their stories from people who have sought them out. In a way, you are making their jobs easier.

When you secure publicity, send the clippings to those colleagues, clients, and referral sources who have an interest in the subject matter. Be careful that you don't appear to be merely self-serving by sending people information in which they have no interest. And while relevant press can positively impact your brand and exposure, be very careful not to reveal anything you don't want your boss, clients, or referral sources to see in print. Print lasts forever. If you do not ask a reporter to go "off the record," everything you say is fair game.

Another effective self-promotion strategy is the receipt of recognition. Obtaining accolades, credentials, awards, and making certain lists builds credibility and can lead to new relationships and business opportunities. Luckily, there is no shortage of such opportunities. For example, Martindale-Hubbell is the primary listing and rating organization for lawyers. It employs a three-tier rating systems: (i) Rated, (ii) BV Distinguished, and (iii) AV Preeminent. Focus on your rating immediately with the goal of becoming AV rated as quickly as possible.

The legal industry is notoriously adept at having all kinds of lists and awards. The two I focused on initially were "Up and Comer" and "Rising Star." Find relevant lists and get yourself on them. Many of the lists for which you may qualify at the outset of your career are usually nothing more than popularity contests, but clients and referral sources usually do not know that. Awards and accolades have a snowball effect, and the more you have, the better positioned you will be for more selective acknowledgements, like being listed in Chambers .

Achieving recognition and accolades is nice, but it's relatively ineffective unless appropriately leveraged. Befriend the marketing person at your firm, and in a tactful manner ask for his or her help to maximize coverage and publicity. See how your mentors and other colleagues have successfully marketed similar accomplishments.

Another effective strategy is to contact potential referral sources who also achieved the same recognition. Write notes congratulating them and suggest that you connect for coffee or lunch to explore developing a mutually beneficial relationship.

Step 3 - Accelerate Growth

It's very difficult to develop a significant book of business without being proficient in your chosen profession. If you are a twenty-five-year-old attorney meeting with a fifty-year-old CEO, you will have to overcome the perception that you lack the appropriate experience. Because my experience and prowess lagged behind my ambition, I've dealt with this all of my professional career. If you cannot demonstrate adequate expertise, you will embarrass yourself and your firm. After all, clients are seeking your professional advice to solve a business problem, pursue an opportunity, ensure compliance, or address some other critical matter that requires expertise they do not possess. You would not think too highly of a surgeon who could not adequately describe the operation your family member was undergoing no matter how affable, funny, or charismatic he was.

Because there are many gray issues, it takes professional service providers years to gain significant expertise. Being a skilled advisor requires the application of malleable principles to a dynamic set of facts. Thus, experience is a critical aspect of being a successful professional service provider. That is why there is generally a seven to ten-year track to becoming a partner or managing director, and you rarely see someone immediately out of college or graduate school leading engagements. No matter how intelligent or naturally gifted someone may be, when it comes to providing sophisticated advice, experience is a key element to proficiency. That does not mean, however, that you should sit back and wait seven to ten years before implementing a business development strategy. With a little proactivity and determination, you can bend the learning curve to expedite the acquisition of relevant knowledge.

Bend the Learning Curve

In order to more rapidly achieve the financial rewards and independence adjunct to being a rainmaker, you need to accelerate your knowledge of, and experience in, your chosen profession. A good initial step is to demonstrate to your boss and other senior colleagues that you are ambitious and intent on learning, growing, and expanding your skill set. Next, you must proactively seek out new and challenging tasks and volunteer for assignments, many of which may not be related to a specific client engagement. Complete these assignments quickly and accurately.

Regularly read relevant industry journals and prepare summaries of important developments for your colleagues and clients. Attend seminars, take classes online or at a local university, and read books to expand your knowledge of relevant subjects. Pitch senior colleagues on an idea for an article or presentation and then ghostwrite the materials. Researching and writing an article on a specific topic is a great way to enhance your knowledge. But before selecting a topic, keep the goal in mind, which is to add value by focusing on relevant subjects and offering practical solutions, not waxing philosophical on some highly nuanced issue just to demonstrate your intellectual superiority.

Another great way to expedite the experiential curve is to volunteer in relevant community organizations, non-profits, or charitable organizations. For example, if you are a litigation attorney, volunteer to represent pro bono defendants. Since there is a shortage of help, you will likely get an overwhelming amount of responsibility relative to your current level of experience. Become a board member of a not-for-profit, take on important tasks, and learn from (and build relationships with) more experienced board members. Being on a not-for-profit board is a great opportunity to make a positive contribution while gaining relevant experience. Another avenue is teaching a course at a nearby college, graduate school, or even online.

While you are proving yourself to your colleagues and developing relevant skills on non-client matters, take full advantage of every opportunity to interact directly with clients. These offer occasions for tremendous growth and advancement. Focus on delivering exceptional service and being proactive. If you prove yourself to your firm's clients, you will gain more responsibility directly from them since they are often eager to have you complete their work at a much lower rate than your more senior colleagues. Your supervising partners will be reluctant to take away an assignment given to you directly by a client, even if they think it's over your head, for fear of angering the client or creating a negative impression.

When interfacing directly with clients, impress them with specific knowledge regarding their situation and be incredibly responsive. It is extremely frustrating for a client if you are unfamiliar with the history and facts of the engagement. They do not care that you may be filling in for another colleague or have just been recently assigned to their project. Clients who are paying hundreds of dollars per hour are irritated when they perceive that young, inexperienced, and unprepared professionals are being trained on their dime and wasting their valuable time. The opposite is equally true. Clients appreciate a smart, hard-working, and well-informed young professional. The following personal story underscores this point.

Early in my career when I was practicing law, I worked on a very contentious restructuring. Our firm represented a Fortune 500 company that was in an epic battle with one of its largest resellers. The dispute was so intense that it quickly became the only thing I worked on; it continued that way for nearly two years.

I will never forget a major hearing my boss and I were tirelessly preparing for all weekend. On Monday, our client flew to Miami with over ten representatives because the issue at stake had significant and far-reaching implications. At 7:00 p.m. the night before the hearing, our client was packing up to go from our office to the hotel. The general counsel for our client, an extremely impressive and senior attorney, asked my boss a question about an issue we had not yet considered. Without skipping a beat, my boss told the general counsel we would research the issue and draft a memo. My boss then shot me the "what are you waiting for?" expression.

I was exhausted, having worked all weekend, but dug deep and stayed up all night researching the issue and drafting that memo. I went home to shower and came back to the office at 7:30 a.m.; our client arrived soon thereafter. As we packed our briefcases to head to court, the general counsel seemed like he just remembered a distant thought. He turned to my boss and asked if we had researched the issue he mentioned. My boss handed him my memo.

The general counsel was floored. He jokingly told my boss in front of a dozen people that he wanted to hire me, but the look he gave me said it all. He genuinely appreciated my Herculean effort, and that was a turning point in my relationship with that client, my boss, and my firm. My client started contacting me directly with assignments and entrusting me with hearings, depositions, and other important matters. His confidence in me rubbed off on my boss and other colleagues and created an upward spiral.

The most fulfilling aspect was that after the case concluded, our Fortune 500 client reached out to me directly with new matters, and my boss was gracious about sharing some of the origination credit with me. That's when it clicked—that delivering exceptional client service and making their needs paramount would be rewarded by more responsibility, trust, and continued business opportunities.

Specialize

You cannot be everything to everybody. In the same way a brain surgeon would not perform a knee replacement operation, professional services involve many layers of specialization. It would be highly unusual for an attorney to be equally skilled at litigating a business dispute, composing a purchase agreement to acquire a company, leading a Chapter 11 restructuring, and drafting wills and trusts.

As you gain more experience and begin to feel more comfortable with your macro-specialization, whether it is middle market investment banking, auditing public companies, or business litigation, you should begin developing expertise on discrete topics within your area of excellence. To identify sub-specialties, focus on complex topics that interest you that appear in engagements with some level of frequency. For example, when I was a corporate restructuring attorney, I developed an expertise in the mechanics of distressed M&A transactions, such as the sale of companies under Section 363 of the Bankruptcy Code. To gain more experience, I volunteered to work on deals within my firm that involved M&A transactions. I also read numerous books and attended classes on corporate finance.

Be prudent and avoid devoting your time to novel issues that may rarely impact future clients. After you have developed some expertise with one or more relevant sub-specialties, write articles for trade journals, create or contribute to a blog, speak at conferences, educate your colleagues on industry developments, and seek out every opportunity within your firm to work on such matters. This is a great way to distinguish yourself amongst your clients and peers.

Get on Your Cycle

AS WE HAVE WITNESSED in the last few years, economic swings can occur abruptly. Market conditions change, which may impact the demand for your specialty. The effect can last for months or years. For example, if you are a real estate lawyer, and your sole expertise is representing developers in Florida, you were likely very exposed during the real estate meltdown in that state in the 2008 timeframe.

Accordingly, it is prudent to be vigilant of macro-economic trends impacting your specialization and to take appropriate measures to mitigate the impact of market conditions on your livelihood. By developing counter-cyclical expertise, you will hedge your downside when market conditions change, and you will also become a more well-rounded service provider. For example, I have developed expertise in healthy M&A to counterbalance my considerable experience working with underperforming businesses as the demand for these services vacillates with economic conditions. I have a friend who is a real estate development lawyer in Florida who shrewdly developed skills and experience representing buyers and sellers of distressed real estate assets. While his colleagues were making less money and worrying about job security during the downturn, he was thriving by representing opportunistic buyers and lenders with portfolios of distressed assets.

Keep in mind that the best time to acquire a new, counter-cyclical skill set is when you do not need it. Waiting until the next market crash will leave you unprepared to seize the opportunity.

Broaden Your Horizons

WE DO NOT PROVIDE professional services in a vacuum. A well-rounded and trusted advisor, regardless of his or her specialization, understands the various implications of a particular business situation, including legal, regulatory, operational, financial, and otherwise. He or she needs to be able to see the big picture from 20,000 feet as well as from the weeds. Think about the quarterback of a football team. He not only calls the plays and leads the offense, but he knows what every offensive player in every position should be doing at any given moment. That is why he is generally the highest paid player on the team.

You want to be the trusted advisor calling the shots, identifying important issues, and recommending professional contacts to help resolve them. However, before you can appreciate the entire landscape of your client's situation, you must have a good working knowledge of your clients, as well as related specializations that are often implicated. For example, as investment bankers focused on sell-side M&A, the majority of our assignments revolved around selling companies. As investment bankers, we need to understand business basics:

- how they operate, develop, and deliver products or services
- financial statement analysis
- customer, competitor, and industry dynamics
- key performance indicators
- legal and regulatory issues
- capital structures
- internal and external drivers that impact performance

Simply knowing how to create a leverage buyout model and a buyer's list with no real understanding of the inner mechanics of a company is extremely limiting.

As I encourage my younger colleagues, a well-rounded investment banker should also be able to add value in related areas, such as in connection with the drafting and negotiation of the documents memorializing the transaction. Our clients and their attorneys appreciate the second set of eyes and team approach to producing the best outcome.

Think about additional ways you can add value to your clients. If you are a business lawyer, learn how to read and analyze financial statements. If you are an auditor on the front line of your client's performance, learn the basics of insolvency and restructuring strategies if their businesses are underperforming. Clients greatly appreciate when you add value outside your core expertise. It also provides a great bonding opportunity with other service providers— one built on trust and mutual respect. The best time to build relationships with other professionals is when you are in the trenches together, speaking frequently, and working collaboratively to engender a successful outcome for your mutual client. A collaborative team approach generally leads to better outcomes for clients, and, therefore, greater potential for repeat business with that client and their service providers.

In sum, developing skills in related areas will enable you to offer more value to your clients and lead you one step closer to the ultimate goal of becoming a trusted advisor. Once that happens, your clients and referral sources will not only begin referring you more work, they will be eager to refer their friends and colleagues.

Market Knowledge

Clients and referral partners are impressed by professionals who are well informed about relevant industry developments, news, and trends, especially if such tidbits of knowledge items are not generally well-known. Read relevant newspapers, business magazines, and trade publications; follow reliable and insightful information sources on social media; and attend relevant industry seminars, trade shows, and networking events. Immerse yourself in the network that encircles your specialty to gain proprietary knowledge and market intelligence.

For example, if you are an investment banker focused on sell-side M&A, you should consistently follow and meet with middle-market private equity firms, banks, non-traditional lenders, and corporate M&A lawyers to discuss what they are working on as well as their view of the market, valuations, current leverage, and deal terms. Being active in your industry and deal community is the best way to stay ahead of any changes in market conditions. This type of proprietary knowledge is exceedingly valuable and will differentiate you from your competitors.

Step 4 - Define and Build Your Network

At this point in the process, you have enhanced your personal brand and image, gained some practical knowledge and experience, implemented strategies to be more likeable, and are well-informed about industry dynamics and relevant marketplace developments. You are almost ready to have productive discussions with potential referral sources and clients. It is natural to have trepidations, but rest assured, it is very common to involve another colleague with more relevant expertise when pitching a client on professional services. Do not feel like you need to know everything—and resist the urge to pretend that you do. You simply need to spot issues, answer basic questions, convey confidence, and articulate your value proposition as to how beneficial you or your firm can be.

You should also be prepared to answer basic questions regarding your firm, the background of other team members, experience in the relevant industry, billing practices, and rates. If you do not know the answer to a question, write it down and tell the person you will get back to him or her shortly. To hone your skills and assess your readiness, practice role playing with your family, significant other, or a good friend. Have someone act out the part of an interested client by asking you tough questions. This will be a good barometer regarding your readiness and will help you build confidence. I know this sounds goofy, but it is considerably less traumatizing than embarrassing yourself in front of a client.

Once you've done this, you are almost ready to be turned loose to start your networking efforts in earnest. You just need to know two fundamental things: to whom and how you should market, which will be the subject of the next few sections.

Who Is Your Target Market?

Partners and marketing personnel frequently encourage young professionals within their firms to "network more." Of course, this offers little practical guidance and raises questions such as, "With whom should I network?" and "How do I effectively network?" Following this advice blindly can prove to be frustrating and highly inefficient. As professionals and service providers, your most valuable asset is your time. It must be carefully managed. Since your time outside of the office during "normal hours" is limited, you need to develop an effective networking strategy to ensure maximum return on investment. Showing up at overcrowded functions without a cogent strategy is like setting off to sail around the world without a map.

You must be strategic about identifying appropriate networking partners. This starts with an analysis of your target market, which includes the type of clients you are trying to generate through your marketing efforts, and those who can benefit from your services. To be effective, you need to carefully define who and where they are and what they do. Is your target client a person, business, municipality, or not-for-profit? What is your target client's core activity? Do they manufacture products, deliver services, build hotels, or develop software? Where is your target client based? Does it operate locally, regionally, or nationally? Does it have multiple employees or just a few? Is it a small start-up, mid-size, or large enterprise? Privately owned or public? Healthy or distressed?

For example, your target *market* may be healthcare providers with revenues of $25 to $250 million that are located in the Northeast. Your target market may be not-for-profit organizations focused on social welfare issues in Chicago, or middle-market service providers based in California. As you refine your definition of your target market, identify the most appropriate type of *contacts* within such markets. That person may be the CEO, CFO, general counsel, chief technology officer, VP of human resources, or hold a myriad of other positions. You generally want to avoid mid-level gatekeepers and market directly to the ultimate decision maker, located at the intersection of your target market and target contact.

Befriend Trusted Advisors

ONCE YOU HAVE DEFINED your target client, consider the types of people who are in frequent contact with, and have influence over, your target client.

Why? Because professional services are too important to an organization to be acquired without an appropriate recommendation from a trusted source. When an executive is served with a multi-million dollar lawsuit, or a business owner receives an unsolicited offer to acquire his company for $100 million, they generally do not search Google or hire someone who has just made a cold call. Professional services engagements are often referred by a *trusted advisor*, who is frequently an attorney, wealth manager, accountant, or other professional who has established a powerful relationship predicated upon mutual trust and respect.

Most business executives maintain a small group of trusted advisors to whom they turn when they need objective advice on how to handle complex and important situations. The trusted advisor acts as a *consigliore* to executives and business owners and exerts tremendous influence over them. As a result of the trusted advisor's track record of delivering reliable, unbiased, and helpful advice in the past, he or she has a unique level of influence. When you are referred to a potential client by its trusted advisor, you have automatic credibility. In essence, the trusted advisor is staking his or her reputation on the referral and is vouching for you. There is a powerful inference of trust that is demonstrated by the following set of relationships: Janet (business owner) trusts Bob (attorney), and Bob trusts you; therefore, Janet trusts you.

As you will soon appreciate, the cornerstone of an effective business development strategy for any professional is to have strong relationships with as many trusted advisors as possible, with the goal of ultimately becoming a trusted advisor to executives, referral sources and business owners.

While having strong relationships with trusted advisors will open the floodgates for referrals, there are simply not that many advisors who reach that status. Further, it's often not clear at the outset of a relationship whether Bob is simply Janet's attorney or Janet's trusted advisor. If the former, Bob's influence over Janet may be limited. If the latter, and he is truly a trusted advisor, whomever Bob refers has a high likelihood of being retained, assuming his or her skill set and compensation are commensurate with the need.

As a result of these nuances, especially at the formative stages of your business development strategy implementation, you should not limit yourself when trying to identify trusted advisors. They will ultimately shake out of your broader network. As such, your initial goal is to build a network of high caliber professionals that regularly offer complementary products or services to your target clients and have the potential to be trusted advisors. I refer to these professionals as your *target referral sources*, of which trusted advisors is a discreet and valuable subset.

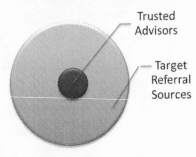

Target Referral Sources

THESE PROFESSIONALS GENERALLY OFFER non-competitive, complementary products or services to your target clients. For example, if you are a management consultant focused on providing operational enhancement solutions to large-cap public companies in the oil and gas sector, and you are typically retained by a chief financial officer, think about who consistently provides professional services to these companies and has the ear of decision makers. You may conclude that your target clients frequently rely on advice from their corporate attorney, accountant, and investment banker. These individuals would be your target referral sources (see diagram below). Since your target client may work with a number of lawyers or accountants from the same firm, you typically want to focus your efforts on the attorney or accountant with the best relationship with your target client's most senior executive.

The List

IT IS NOW TIME to sit down and develop a list of individuals that meet your criteria of target clients and target referral sources. Start with your target clients and list anyone you know who is directly associated with the person or organization—friends, family, or colleagues may come to mind. In the early stages of your career, your list of target clients and ability to effectively market to them will be limited, so turn your attention to target referral sources. Start by casting a wide net. List all professionals you know who may come in contact with target clients and who you perceive to be trusted advisors to them. This can include business colleagues, friends from college or graduate school, members of your place of worship, family members, or loosely connected friends via Facebook, Twitter, LinkedIn or other social networking sites.

Consider professionals who are older than you as they are much more likely to be trusted advisors. My best referral sources are ten to twenty years older than me, so don't be intimidated by someone's age. Established rainmakers are savvy marketers, and they will look at you as a source of connection to a generation in which they have few useful contacts. Plus, if you can refer them business, they will not care that you are twenty years younger. Finally, think outside the box to identify anyone who may have a strong relationship with, and the respect of, target clients, such as physicians, personal trainers, real estate agents, or restaurant owners.

As you are creating this list of potential target referral sources, keep in mind that in addition to meeting your criteria based on service offering, geography, and other factors, it is critical that you only include people whom you and others hold in very high regard. For example, a dentist may be consistently in touch with your target clients, but if someone in your target client does not consider that person a trusted business advisor, you are not making the most efficient use of your time.

And on another note: avoid the temptation to include someone on your list whom you consider of mediocre talent or reputation. It can negatively impact your brand. It's guilt by association. The converse is also true, which is why it's important to associate with high-caliber professionals—because they will boost your brand.

Don't Overlook Your Co-Workers

IT MAY NOT SEEM immediately apparent, but some of the best people to build relationships with are down the hall or in another office of your firm. Many professional service firms employ the concept of *shared origination* to account for the sharing of business development credit. Build relationships with the key rainmakers within your practice group. Gain the trust of partners with whom you frequently work by being accountable, making them look good with their clients, and making their lives easier by efficiently handling the grunt work. They will increasingly rely on you to interact directly with clients and are more likely to be generous with shared origination credit. In addition, target professionals within your firm in different practice groups. If corporate and real estate attorneys are great referral sources for you, build relationships with these professionals within your firm and share origination credit. I know a number of professionals who dramatically boost their annual income by consistently generating a lot of shared revenue origination.

There is another important reason to build strong relationships with your colleagues. The professional services industry is highly transient; it is typical for professionals to move among firms several times throughout their careers. If they ever leave the firm at which you are currently both employed, you could be perfectly positioned to inherit their clients or obtain referrals from them at their new firm. Professionals frequently leave to go in-house, which means they may be in a position to hire you. As such, you should treat *all* of your colleagues as potential target clients and target referral sources. You should also make a concerted effort to build relationships with influential members of your firm regardless of cross-sell opportunities. By impressing senior level colleagues with your capabilities, drive and enthusiasm, you will be exposed to more opportunities and advancement within your firm.

Expand Your Network with Stars

WHILE ALL YOUR NETWORKING efforts should be focused on high-caliber people, you should devote some of your time to meeting the stars—the top ten percent of the top ten percent. These are super high-performers, generally forty years old and under, who are innovative, active in politics and their community, are already running companies, and have achieved an unusual level of success and influence at an early age. These people are frequently in the press and identified in lists, such as the Forty Under 40. Many of them may not neatly fit within your definition of target client or target referral sources, which is okay because emerging leaders generally have amazing contacts and a lot of influence over them. So, the goal is to befriend and add value to them and their network.

That said, it is generally challenging to meet and build relationships with young stars. Unlike target referral sources who generally welcome the opportunity to meet other professionals, emerging leaders need a reason to meet with a lawyer, investment banker, accountant, or consultant. To justify the meeting, you need to be prepared to articulate how you can add demonstrable value. My personal experience with an organization called

Leaders of Tomorrow provides an example of how to creatively accomplish this goal.

Leaders of Tomorrow

AFTER PRACTICING RESTRUCTURING LAW for several years with a prominent law firm, it became readily apparent to me that the handful of attorneys who generated significant business played by different rules than the average attorney. Setting aside the obvious (their income), they were more autonomous and influential. After recognizing this dynamic, I was eager to start developing business; however, I quickly realized there was a small problem—I did not have many relationships with high caliber professionals or executives, nor did I have much expertise as a restructuring lawyer.

I started attending large networking events and was soon frustrated by the frenzy of low-level company representatives mindlessly handing out business cards. I found this type of networking unfocused and a complete waste of time. I wanted to meet extremely successful executives as well as like-minded, highly ambitious young professionals; and apropos of my typical impatience, I wanted to do it quickly. However, "wanting" to do it was not going to make it magically come to fruition. Fortunately, I instinctively realized that devising a self-serving strategy would fail, and that I needed to figure out a way to add value to everyone involved.

In an effort to learn from their successes and missteps, I've always been interested in reading about highly successful business leaders. I thought that ambitious young professionals probably shared the same curiosity. This prompted me to start an organization called Leaders of Tomorrow, an invitation-only group premised on mentoring the next generation of business and community leaders in South Florida. The idea was to secure highly successful business leaders to speak with and mentor a handpicked group of young leaders in an intimate setting. While it sounds easy, like most successful ventures analyzed with the benefit of hindsight, LOT was initially quite challenging. I solicited the assistance of another young attorney at my firm who shared a similar mindset and objective. We were surprised by the initial resistance we encountered. Our strategy for attracting young leaders was to write and call CEOs of the top companies (except professional service firms) in South Florida, and ask them to recommend their top performer under forty years old for membership, regardless of that person's specialization. In retrospect, the CEOs and business leaders were skeptical and probably thought we were recruiters. Potential under-forty candidates were also leery, probably because we had no track record, and they were frequently solicited to get involved with charities and serve on not-for-profit boards.

Attracting speakers was also challenging since we were targeting high caliber people who generally only spoke at events at which they were being either paid or honored. Our pitch to potential speakers was that we had identified a select group of South Florida's next generation of young business and community leaders, and the guest would have a rare opportunity to meet with them and provide insights, guidance, and mentorship.

Fortunately, the leadership of our law firm completely supported this endeavor and helped us secure our first speaker, a prominent real estate developer named Terry Stiles. Following the event, he was impressed by the quality of our members and asked if we needed assistance finding our next speaker. He asked whether we would like Wayne Huizenga as a speaker, who, as you probably know, is an extraordinarily successful entrepreneur. He is the only person to start three Fortune 500 companies—Blockbuster Entertainment, AutoNation, and Waste Management. We ended up securing him, and he mesmerized our members with the story of how he started his first company (Waste Management) with just a single garbage truck, which he drove. His appearance prompted an article in the *Miami Herald* about Leaders of Tomorrow, and then the group's popularity exploded. Finding young leaders to participate was no longer a problem. In fact, to maintain a consistent experience of only high caliber young professionals, we started turning people away.

Leaders of Tomorrow provided a unique value proposition: members were able to interact with an extraordinarily successful business leader in an intimate setting as well as an opportunity to meet other rising young leaders. I played the ambassador role during and between our quarterly events, generating goodwill by introducing members to each other. I earned their respect and trust by delivering value to all involved. The speakers appreciated the opportunity to give back to their community and influence the next generation of young leaders in South Florida as well. It was a massive win-win.

LOT taught me so much, including the fact that like-minded, achievement-oriented individuals like to associate and build relationships with each other, especially when there is a common business or civic goal that's being advanced. That is why the world is filled with premier and exclusive clubs and conferences such as YPO, YEO, World Economic Forum, TED, and many others. By starting an organization, you get to invite members you want to meet and be at the center of it all. You will gain favor for creating a forum that others find valuable and fulfilling.

Ours was a very successful venture and helped me build long, lasting relationships. It was also a great opportunity for my former law firm to gain exposure to influential young professionals and seasoned executives. I encourage you to create strategies to meet superstars. Whether it's organizing your own Leaders of Tomorrow, hosting events for local or national politicians, becoming active in your alumni association or local country club, serving on a board, or raising money for a not-for-profit, put yourself in a leadership position to maximize your exposure and make a difference. It will demonstrate ambition and innovation and enable you to develop leadership skills. Whatever you decide to do, make sure you are consistent and passionate about it; otherwise, your insincerity will be palpable, and you will waste your time.

Conferences and Organizations

CONFERENCES CAN BE A highly effective way to harvest new relationships and nurture existing ones. A good industry conference is like shooting fish in a barrel; it will have a high concentration of target referral sources in a single location, all of whom will be open to networking. Yet many young professionals treat conferences as a boondoggle, even if only on a subconscious level. Simply showing up at a conference with no plan and hoping to bump into target referral sources is a waste of your time and your firm's money. Conversely, the best thought-out strategy will be of little value if you have selected an incongruous conference.

Because they are being marketed to you and your colleagues all day long, identifying relevant industry conferences should be relatively easy. The harder part is determining which is the best one for you given your time constraints. Research the conferences you have identified and discuss them with people within your industry and firms whom you respect.

After identifying an appropriate conference, attempt to get involved. Start by reaching out to the person who is organizing the event and volunteer to speak, serve on a panel, or otherwise add value. This is one of the best ways to establish yourself as an expert and a leader in front of a room full of potential referral sources. You are afforded special status as a speaker, and if you are prepared and provide valuable insights, people will seek out opportunities to meet you. If you are unable to secure a speaking engagement because you are not perceived as having sufficient expertise, find a partner in your firm and pitch him or her the idea—and then offer to write the material.

If you cannot identify an opportunity to make a substantive contribution to the conference, volunteer to help with organizing it. Conference organizers usually welcome help with the details, follow-up, and logistics of the event. This is a great way to build a relationship with the organizing association and to get an inside look at important attendees you may want to meet. It provides you with an excuse to introduce yourself to attendees and gives you a sense of belonging as opposed to showing up and not knowing anyone.

A few weeks prior to the conference, you should reach out to colleagues, speakers, and other people you want to meet, and explain why it may be mutually beneficial to have a brief meeting. You should set up several specific meetings throughout the day—coffee, breakfast, lunch, and dinner. A strategy that I often use at conferences is hosting my own dinner. Approximately one month before a conference, I start reaching out to a diverse group of highly regarded professionals who could benefit by knowing each other, and I invite them to dinner. I frequently join forces with a colleague at another professional services firm (in a related field), so that we can both invite different contacts and assure we all meet new people. Plus, it helps to split the bill if your firm is skeptical about paying for the event. Be mindful of the conference's formal dinner, so you are not competing with it. Similar to Leaders of Tomorrow, you are now the center of influence, connecting people and exponentially increasing your reciprocal goodwill. Make sure you are well prepared regarding the background of all the guests, so you can facilitate helpful introductions at dinner. For example:

You: Joe, it's great seeing you. Do you know Judy Dealhound?

Joe: Great to see you, too. No, I don't know Judy.

You: I will introduce you—you need to know each other. Judy's a lawyer focusing on representing real estate investment funds. She's not only a great lawyer but also sees some unique deal opportunities.

Joe: That would be great; we're always looking for off-market deals.

You: Judy, I want to introduce you to a friend, Joe Vulture. Joe is a partner at a real estate investment fund that specializes in acquiring and repositioning distressed assets. They're always looking for proprietary and interesting deals.

The key to this and any other introduction is to frame it up as mutually beneficial. If you leave out the part that Judy often sees proprietary deals, then it appears that the relationship can only be one way—Joe hiring Judy for legal work. If Judy is shrewd, she'll emphasize her ability to uncover off-market investment opportunities.

When you meet new people at the dinner or conference, you must get in touch with them within a few days and then keep them in your follow-up rotation. Prompt follow-up is a critical facet of business development as it is usually the first indicia of evidence to your target referral source that you are responsible and sincere. Meeting someone once is generally not going to lead to a referral or business; a relationship has to be cultivated, and you should take the first step.

Step 5 - Work Your Network

At this point, you have assembled an initial list of target clients and target referral sources, which I will refer to as your network. This is a great start and your foundation, but like cement sitting in a barrel, it's of little use in building the career of your dreams unless properly used. Leveraging the power of your network is not rocket science, but it requires the consistent implementation of an effective strategy, which revolves around building and growing mutually beneficial relationships with network members. In order to do so, you must approach networking with the mindset of not only reciprocity but altruism.

In all facets of your life, you should focus on bringing something to the relationship table (as waiters bring food *to* a table) as opposed to just taking from it (as busboys take food *from* a table). Adding value is an essential element of powerful business relationships that most people fail to grasp. If you approach business development as a way to generate clients from other people without giving anything in return, you will inevitably fail, or at best, not reach your full potential. In building professional relationships, you must take a long-term view, focus on helping your friends and contacts succeed, be a genuine and trusted advisor, and give more than you receive. Remember to always be the waiter and never forget that you are not selling the next greatest Apple device; you are selling a skill set that many people possess and that clients increasingly view as a commodity.

One question I'm frequently asked by younger colleagues is, "How do you generate business for your referral sources when you have no business opportunities to refer to them?" Simply put: add value in another way. Whether it is a relevant introduction, supporting someone's political fundraiser or charity event, helping someone find a new job, organizing a regular networking event, serving as a recommendation, provide your expertise at no expense; the specific act is less important than the intended purpose of that act, which is to help someone else achieve his or her goals. I've encouraged some of my junior colleagues to offer their investment banking expertise to their cohorts at law firms who can benefit greatly from their knowledge of finance and market terms. Junior M&A attorneys may not be comfortable calculating working capital or other financial metrics in a purchase agreement, so this is a ripe opportunity for an investment banking analyst or associate to add value.

Identify Opportunities

The trick to adding value to your network is to become adept at uncovering issues, challenges, or problems that your target referral sources and target clients are experiencing. These issues provide opportunities for your network and help both parties if the issue is properly resolved. For example, let's assume you are an investment banker, and that you're having lunch with a colleague who owns a fifty-store restaurant chain. You ask him how his business is doing, and he provides the typical answer, "It's going fine."

You need to penetrate deeper and give him a reason to open up by showing genuine interest and demonstrating relevant knowledge indicating you may have some constructive ideas. You say, "As a result of work I'm doing with another client, I recently became aware that food costs have skyrocketed. How has that impacted your business?" Mr. Restaurant Entrepreneur says, "As a matter of fact, our food costs have doubled, and our lease rates have recently increased, which has caused several locations to significantly under-perform. Also, we just got a whopping bill from our auditor that's causing a cash crunch in itself."

You now have an opening to solve an important issue. You should immediately follow up to obtain more relevant information, such as learning how many restaurants he operates, how many are under-performing, and whether each location is separately owned. Now you've identified a problem that you can help solve. You ask him whether he has spoken with a restructuring lawyer who can potentially help him with the underperforming locations and his overall capital structure. If he says no, you can suggest the most appropriate target referral source, both in terms of their relevant skill and experience and their likelihood of referring you work in the future.

After your meeting, you call the restructuring attorney to share a little about the situation and to tell him to expect a call—but do not forget the softball Mr. Restaurant Entrepreneur threw you: he is displeased with his accounting firm. You should offer to introduce him to an appropriate member of your network. You have now created goodwill with Mr. Restaurant Entrepreneur, a future client and referral source, by helping him solve two problems, and created goodwill with a restructuring attorney and accountant, who are in a position to refer you business. Plus, you may even create an opportunity for yourself if the lease restructuring is unsuccessful, and your colleague decides to sell the restaurant chain. This dynamic is so powerful. I often spend time on calls and in meetings discussing business issues, which I am confident will not result in an assignment for my firm, but might potentially uncover an opportunity for one of my target referral sources.

You should also be mindful of non-business problems that you can address. For example, I was meeting with a potential client who was relocating his business to South Florida. I asked how he was going to transition his family, where he was going to live, and whether he needed help in that regard. He indicated that he was having problems finding a house. I offered to introduce him to a good friend who is a realtor. This type of problem solving grows goodwill within your network and will also be rewarded. The more people to whom you offer solutions, the more people will trust your advice and counsel. This is the path to becoming a trusted advisor.

Take Action

WHAT DO YOU ENJOY doing? Going to sporting events, eating at nice restaurants, drinking cocktails, going to concerts, playing pool, boating, running, yoga, attending business seminars? Whatever it is, start doing that on a consistent basis with members of your network. I enjoy going to breakfast with colleagues because, in addition to liking food, I am a morning person and find people less uptight early in the day and more open since they are just starting their day and are not yet impacted by stressors.

Nurturing professional relationships in settings you enjoy and in which you feel comfortable accelerates this process of building genuine bonds. However, do not lose sight that there is a purpose for the meeting other than having fun. It is to explore ways to develop a mutually beneficial professional relationship. If you do not believe that there is a strong possibility that this can happen with a target referral source, you should not have the meeting. Despite the enjoyable setting, remember this is work, not play time.

You should always prepare for a meeting with a target referral source. Read the person's profile on his or her firm's website; review their LinkedIn, Facebook, and other social media accounts to see whether you share any common relationships or interests; and Google them to uncover any press or relevant information. Finding some type of commonality such as a shared friend, school, or passion is a great way to establish rapport.

When you meet, it is incumbent upon you to understand their ideal clients and relevant experience while representing them. Likewise, you should concisely explain how you define your target clients, relevant experience, and unique value proposition. More than anything, you need to embody the new brand you developed while being extremely likeable. Since your target referral source is essentially your marketing agent, it is imperative that you leave a good impression.

In addition to understanding your target referral

source's ideal target client, you also should understand the types of referral sources that are most helpful. Near the end of each meeting, suggest a couple of introductions that meet the criteria of his or her target referral source. If you have adequately prepared for the meeting and are constantly growing your network, you will have a couple of introductions in mind. Make sure they are quality introductions since the person you introduce is a reflection of your brand and may be the sole barometer of how you are currently adding value to this relationship. Ask your colleague to do the same. Be clear about the type of people you want to meet and how they fit within your definition of target clients or target referral sources.

Following your meeting, take the first step and make a high-caliber introduction. Immediate follow-up positively reinforces your sincere desire to build a mutually beneficial relationship. When you get back to your office, send a simple email introduction along the following lines:

> *Kevin…I had lunch with my friend, Susan Jones, earlier today and thought about you. Susan provides management consulting services to Fortune 1000 companies and has some great clients and innovative ideas. Since you focus on providing services to similar companies, I thought you guys would enjoy meeting and sharing ideas.*

> *Susan…As I mentioned at lunch, Kevin Anderson is a great guy and a really talented corporate attorney. Unlike many attorneys, he is dealmaker, not a deal breaker, and is extremely creative. He is my "go to" corporate attorney.*

> *I would really encourage you two to get together to discuss ways you can develop a mutually beneficial relationship. At a minimum, you will enjoy getting to know each other.*

If you continue to ask people with whom you are building relationships for a couple of quality introductions, your network will grow exponentially. You should ask all of your relationships to introduce you to anyone who fits within your definition of a target client or target referral source, including friends, classmates from college and graduate school, former colleagues, members of social organizations/charities, family and family friends, and your kids' parents. As long as you continue to add value to your network, your target referral sources will comply.

High-Yield Activity

In my experience, nothing can take the place of one-on-one relationship building. But because this time can be limiting, I like to engage in business development activities that are highly leverageable. These are situations where I can add value to many members of my network at the same time. For example, speaking at conferences, organizing events, and hosting dinners. I encourage you to think creatively. One of my colleagues developed a program to teach lawyers the basics of M&A and valuing companies. He had it certified for CLE credits, then we delivered it to several law firms, and each session included ten or more corporate attorneys. It was a very effective business development tool because it accomplished three important objectives:

> ➤ Provided great value to M&A attorneys who are our target referral sources
> ➤ Established us as experts
> ➤ Enabled us to spend quality time with a number of lawyers during each session

Effectively Using Technology

YOU SHOULD CONSTANTLY ADD high-quality people to your network. As you work your way through your initial list of target referral sources, you need to reach out directly to new potential contacts. Meeting new people can be daunting, but that's normal. I'm an introvert by nature and have morphed over the years in relentless pursuit of my goals. You simply have to weigh your fear of meeting a new person against your desire to succeed.

Technology makes it much easier to both connect with strangers and minimize the fear of rejection. You no longer have to walk up to a stranger and introduce yourself. Instead, you can leverage social media and online networking sites by connecting with friends of friends on LinkedIn, Facebook, Twitter, Instagram, and countless other social media networks. Keep in mind that while these technological innovations are great connectivity tools, they cannot and should not replace face-to-face relationship building. Relationships are built over time in person by sharing experiences and stories about your families, careers and aspirations, and by helping each other personally and professionally. This type of person-al bond cannot be replicated by technology alone. As a result, these aids are simply an adjunct to your in-person business development efforts.

When reaching out to someone with whom I do not currently have a relationship, I consistently use email as an effective icebreaker. For example, when I'm planning a business trip to another city, I will contact a prominent corporate restructuring attorney (one of my best referral sources) and ask if I can stop by his or her office for a few minutes to learn more about the practice. I explain that we often work with restructuring attorneys and frequently refer them into transactions. I will let the attorney know that I've heard great things about his or her firm (insert a common contact if you can identify one), and that we've been eager to expand our relationships with a top restruc-turing law firm in Atlanta (or whatever city it may be). I've rarely been denied a meeting and have made many great contacts along the way. I like meeting new people during business trips for three reasons.

> First, it creates a sense of urgency as you are only there for a finite period of time.
> Second, it creates the impression that you are busy serving clients.
> Third, you make the person seem important by carving out time during your tight travel schedule to visit with him or her.

When you meet with a new contact, be sure to apply the principles discussed earlier: listen more than you talk, ask insightful questions, and be prepared. Ask him or her to describe his or her ideal client or business opportunity. Most importantly, resist the urge to launch into a diatribe about your accomplishments and the influential people you know. Instead, demonstrate how you can add value to the relationship—ideally with a live opportunity.

Track and Analyze Performance

It is important to track your activity and analyze performance to ensure that you are both adding to, and receiving value from, your network. Mindless networking is an extraordinary waste of time. There are sophisticated customer relationship management (CRM) solutions, but I suggest keeping it simple initially. I use a spreadsheet to track my activities, categorizing target referral sources by occupation. I use the same spreadsheet to track my performance relative to my revenue goals (see example next page). It is imperative to use your spreadsheet to routinely analyze your performance. As discussed earlier, it is critical to consistently meet revenue and referral goals. Monthly analysis of performance will help you pivot before year-end, when it's too late. You do not want to fall behind on your monthly goals, especially the revenue you are referring to your network. Each revenue cell of the form you create should tie to a separate sheet that indicates the specific sources of the revenue. This will enable you to quantitatively analyze your and your network's performance.

	Revenue Earned	Revenue Referred
2014 GOALS	**$500,000**	**$750,000**
January	$20,000	$20,000
February	$8,325	$30,000
March	$52,500	$12,500
April	$16,560	$5,000
May	$36,424	$2,500
June	$54,435	$64,000
July	$24,375	$18,000
August	$14,312	$42,500
September	$35,000	$18,000
October	-	-
November	-	-
December	-	-
Total	**261,931**	**$212,500**
Performance Relative To Goals	**52%**	**28%**

Prune & Harvest - Repeat

BUILDING A REWARDING NETWORK is not a static exercise; it is an iterative process of expanding and pruning. You should consistently evaluate people based on your impression of their experience, talent, responsiveness, your mutual chemistry, their book of business, and their ability and willingness to consistently refer you business. Focus your efforts on the most prolific rainmakers and trusted advisors, who are often the same people. As your network matures, the takers ("busboys") will become apparent. Regardless of their skill or connections, cease spending time with people who are not reciprocally minded.

As your network expands, you should be mindful of your top target referral sources within each occupational category, both generally and specifically. In other words, if corporate attorneys and wealth managers are important target referral sources, you should endeavor to know as many quality ones you can identify but pay particular attention to the most prolific referrers of business and trusted advisors. Why? Because as you have probably gleaned by now, the secret to generating a lot of referrals is giving a lot of referrals to trusted advisors. If your target referral sources list contains twenty-five wealth managers, it will be difficult to consistently provide referrals to all of them. Providing a referral once every few years is not going to engender a steady flow of referrals back to you. As such, concentrate your efforts on the handful of target referral sources who meet all of the essential criteria:

> Experienced and highly competent advisor whom you feel comfortable referring
> Trusted advisor with influence over their clients and network
> Reciprocally minded with the ability to refer you to target clients and target referral sources
> Someone you like and with whom you enjoy spending time

Stratifying your network is important because it takes a lot of time and energy to develop and maintain deep relationships. It's not feasible to spend consistent, quality time with dozens of people; therefore, it's imperative that you make a conscious effort to spend the most quality time with trusted advisors and your best target referral sources. It's like the 80/20 rule that applies to most businesses: 20% of customers account for 80% of volume. If you want to succeed as a young rainmaker, you've got to have the awareness and confidence to spend your limited business development time with decision makers and people with influence.

Weed Out the Takers and Fakers

You will inevitably come across professionals who are clueless and do not understand that referral relationships are two-way streets. Others, the more insidious type, cloak their true agendas in a veil of altruism. You need to be wary of expending too much time and energy with these "fakers" or succumbing to their chicanery. Nevertheless, the practical reality of business relationships is a bit more nuanced. In the same way that a healthy friendship or relationship with a significant other cannot be guided by a "tit for tat" mindset, neither can networking.

At its core, successful networking is the development of *mutually* beneficial relationships. You should strive to give more than you get and take the first step in referring a potential business opportunity to a high value target referral source. However, because client referrals are the most valuable form of networking currency, you must be prudent not to squander them on people with purely selfish motives. The reason is simple: they are not genuinely interested in seeing you succeed. It is possible that the person to whom you made a referral, despite best intentions, may not have an opportunity to refer you business in six months or even a year. But if there is no reciprocity after a year, or at least genuine attempts such as making relevant introductions, you should have a candid discussion.

It doesn't need to be uncomfortable or confrontational; you simply need to understand "why," so you can determine whether to continue to invest time and effort into the relationship.

For example, assume Bobby Hugedeals is a corporate attorney. Bobby gets referred a lot of work from investment bankers but only gets the opportunity to refer one or two investment banking engagements per year. If Bobby refers those engagements to an investment banker who does not reciprocate, he has wasted two very valuable referrals. More precisely, he has lost two potential engagements that may have been referred to him by a more reciprocally oriented investment banker.

This begs an important question: How do you know whether you are about to refer a valuable assignment to an ungrateful investment banker? If you or your close contacts have no experience with this person, you have to rely on your instincts and make an educated guess. If the person is a trusted advisor and an established rainmaker, he or she likely understands the dynamics of mutually beneficial relationships.

There is, however, the "egomaniac exception," which is not uncommon in professional services. In this instance, the professional believes he is referred a lot of business because he is the most talented investment banker in the world. If so, cross him off your list regardless of his genius because he is unlikely to refer you work, especially when you are in the early stages of your career. If a person claims not to have opportunities to refer you business, you should also cross that name off your list as you've misiden-tified that person as a target referral source.

Sometimes it's not ego or inability; it's simply an over-sight. A few years ago, I sat down with a colleague who was considerably more established and successful. In a non-confrontational manner, I mentioned that I had re-ferred several millions of dollars in business over the last two years and asked why he did not reciprocate. I bluntly asked, "Do you think I'm not capable or qualified?" He was stunned and acknowledged that he was embarrassed that the scales had gotten so out of balance. Within six months of our meeting, he referred two engagements that generated fees in excess of one million dollars.

Be especially vigilant of professionals who appear to be helping, but all of their referrals wind up being dead ends. I call these people "fakers." They are adept at providing introductions to unqualified people or unreliable leads re-garding a potential opportunity, which presents two prob-lems. First, you waste your most precious resource—your time—chasing down and investigating these opportuni-ties. Second, you can be fooled into providing real refer-rals to these fakers, depriving yourself of a return referral from a trusted referral source. It takes a while to uncover these characters, but once you do, limit your time with them.

Step 6 - Find a Mentor

I cannot overemphasize the importance of mentors. They have dramatically changed my career as well as those of my wife (who is a lawyer and law professor) and countless friends. Regardless of how smart, hard-working, or dedicated young professionals may be, experience plays a major role in becoming a successful professional. The value of the advice, guidance, and support that my mentors have provided me throughout my career is immeasurable.

I started my professional career in 1998 as an attorney. I went to law school for the education, thinking it would enable me to become a successful entrepreneur and businessperson. Upon graduating from law school, filled with determination and entrepreneurial spirit, I was ready to conquer the world. To my dismay, the real world was much slower to embrace my self-perceived gifts. The reality is that upon graduation from law school, I had dreams and ambition but not a whole lot more to offer the business world. Since then, I've learned a great deal from my wonderful mentors and from my mistakes when I had the courage and humility to do so.

The circuitous journey that has enabled me to achieve a modicum of success began in my formative years. At an early age, although I could not articulate it then, I instinctively realized that I needed to build mutually beneficial relationships with the most powerful "hoods" in my neighborhood in Queens, which was fraught with public housing projects. I gained their respect on the basketball court, made myself likeable, and provided insights for their latest "business" ventures or help with schoolwork. My childhood taught me that relationships built on mutual trust and respect are just as important, if not more so, than book smarts and innate talents. I would not have survived alone on the latter. This instinct was reinforced early in my career as I stumbled through some unsuccessful business ventures. Luckily, I received help and guidance from some amazing mentors who reinforced the lesson that success in life and in business is due, in large part, to mutually beneficial relationships.

One of those mentors is John Kozyak, a man who helped change the trajectory of my life. John is the founding partner of the prominent firm, Kozyak Tropin & Throckmorton, and one of the most revered and influential attorneys in the country. In 2001, he told me in his infamous deep, raspy voice and slow delivery, "Steve, I know you don't want to be a lawyer, but I think you would really enjoy restructuring companies. With your business acumen, you would be great at it." He suggested that I meet with Paul Singerman, Co-CEO of Berger Singerman, and one of the preeminent corporate restructuring attorneys in the United States. While I had confidence in my abilities as an entrepreneur, strategic thinker, and hard worker, my résumé would have never earned me an interview with a white-shoe law firm like Berger Singerman. I simply did not have the right credentials. Acting on my own, if I had sent my résumé to their recruiting director, I would have likely received a "thanks, but no thanks" form letter.

But a couple of mornings after John emailed his friend, I found myself sitting with Paul at breakfast. I was not convinced that I wanted to practice law, but when he explained that he, too, had a business background and that a great restructuring lawyer must understand the inner workings of his or her clients' business and financial performance, I was intrigued. In late September 2001, Paul's client, Renaissance Cruises, had just filed for protection under Chapter 11 of the Bankruptcy Code. The company, headquartered in Ft. Lauderdale, operated year-round cruise itineraries to the Mediterranean Sea, the Greek Isles, Tahiti and the South Pacific, northern Europe, and Scandinavia. While the company had been experiencing financial difficulties for quite some time, the economic impact resulting from the 9/11 terrorist attacks is credited with its demise.

Paul told me that he could use someone with my business experience on his team. The following week I reported for work at Berger Singerman. I quickly decided that Paul was going to be my mentor whether he liked it or not. I learned a tremendous amount from him about corporate restructuring, business development, negotiating—and how to be an effective lawyer. He demanded complete dedication and perfection, which was not always enjoyable. But he cared about my development and was an amazing mentor, challenging my thinking and pushing my limits. He instilled a visceral desire to perform at the highest level, for which I will always be grateful.

In addition to being a terrific attorney, Paul is a prodigious rainmaker. He generates enough work each year to keep dozens of lawyers busy billing thousands of hours. I studied his business development strategies and have adopted many of them. As they say, "imitation is the sincerest form of flattery."

I used to think of myself proudly as a self-made man who struggled through adversity to achieve professional success and who dreaded asking anyone for help. My father was murdered when I was three months old, my older brother passed away when we were both in our mid-twenties, and my surroundings were volatile at times. I am the first person in my family to graduate from college, and I did not have family or country club relationships to help me along the way.

Several years ago, I finally realized I could not have been more wrong in thinking that I was entirely self-made, and I abandoned the "story" that I created. Most of the things I have accomplished in my life have been a direct result of strong personal relationships, most importantly with my mother, my aunt and uncle, and my wife. I knew this instinctively, but it did not translate into conscious awareness until an epiphany in my mid-thirties revealed that all my success, achievement, and personal growth had been a result of the strength of my personal relationships with family, friends, and mentors.

My success in my investment banking career at Farlie Turner & Co. has been due, in large part, to the relationships I built in the restructuring community during my legal career, and it all started from an email by John Kozyak (who, incidentally, likes my wife immeasurably more than he likes me). I am extremely fortunate that the founders of Farlie Turner, Craig Farlie and Mike Turner, gave me the opportunity, latitude, and extraordinary flexibility to build a new division within their prestigious firm. Without all of this help, encouragement, and guidance from other people, I would not be writing this book because I would have little to offer on the topic of business development or professional success.

Selecting a Mentor

SEEK OUT A MENTOR who has what you desire professionally and personally. It should be someone who is a prodigious rainmaker with strong technical skills and a cheerful disposition. If you are fortunate, you will find one person who embodies all of these traits; if not, seek out separate mentors.

Once you identify potential mentors, devise a strategy to get to know them better. If you do not yet have a strong relationship, volunteer to assist them on a project, ghost-write an article, support their not-for-profit, or any other task that they will perceive as a value-add. Once you build a rapport, let them know you admire their business development capabilities and are curious how they became such successful rainmakers. Ask open-ended questions about what strategies they successfully employ to generate business. What types of people have consistently been their best referral sources, and how have they cultivated relationships with them? What really effective ways have they found to leverage business development efforts—articles, speaking at conferences, organizing events? What mistakes have they made that you can learn from, and what pitfalls should you avoid?

Most professional service providers, especially rainmakers, have well-developed egos and relish the opportunity to discuss themselves and explain why they are so successful. Ask for specific examples, like how they landed client ABC. Pay attention to specific behaviors and qualities these people possess; they are probably unaware of them because they are second nature. For example, Paul

Singerman has an amazing way of making people feel special by giving them his undivided attention.

While you can reap amazing benefits from a great mentor, you should keep in mind that mentorship, like rain-making, is about creating mutually beneficial relationships and genuine connections. Continue to add value to your mentor: show enthusiasm, be accountable, and respect your mentor's time. Otherwise, it will be a short and unfulfilling relationship. Remember that the mentor-mentee relationship is reciprocal and circular, and that one day the mentee becomes the mentor.

CHAPTER 3

Fueling Your Success

The preceding six steps represent the core of your business development plan; however, it is critical to understand that you will not magically be transformed into a rainmaker simply by reading these steps once or practicing them occasionally. These steps represent a new framework of living that should be consistently incorporated in all aspects of your life. As you integrate this new design for living, you will appreciate a constant evolution. Your revenue goals will increase over time, your brand and practical experience will always be growing, and building and enhancing relationships will never end.

Following this blueprint will guide your transformation, but without applying the following principles, your success will be limited. Think about the six-step program as the vehicle that will transport you from point A to point B—from little or no revenue origination and career freedom to rainmaker with lots of freedom and flexibility—and the following suggestions as the high-octane gas that efficiently fuels your journey.

Continuity and Consistency

Target referral sources and target clients forget about you if you do not remain top of mind. As clichéd as "out of sight, out of mind" sounds, it is especially true at the outset of relationships where your marketing message must be repeatedly delivered in order to develop some level of personal brand recognition. These people are busy, and they're preoccupied by their own clients and professional pressures. When asked for a recommendation by a client, they may only have a few moments to consider an appropriate referral. As such, you should be constantly pinging and adding value to your network. You may have a great meeting and chemistry with a target referral source, but in the absence of consistent communication, follow-up, and value-add activities, that connection will be lost in less than a year. They will forget about how competent and charismatic you are unless you remain in regular contact with them.

Continuity of business development effort is one of the single most important things you can do to ensure success. Indeed, the foregoing steps, like most types of knowledge, are useless unless applied. A highly effective and easy way to ensure continuity of effort is to commit to engage in at least one business development initiative each day. It could be a shared meal or drinks, drafting an informative article, making a valuable introduction to a target referral source, sending a potential client relevant information impacting his or her business, or countless other actions. The specific action is not as important as creating the habit of engaging in a value-add business development activity on a daily basis. It can be as simple as sending a brief email such as, "It's been a while since we last connected. How's everything going? Let's get together soon."

I frequently use idle time when waiting in lines, sitting in an airport, pumping gas, or countless other moments to scan my contacts on my phone and send these types of emails or texts. People appreciate your genuine interest in their lives and desire connection.

Initially, you may want to include a daily reminder on your calendar. After doing one business development activity a day for only thirty days, you will begin to develop a routine that comes naturally. Finding time to incorporate business development activities will no longer seem like a burden. It will be like brushing your teeth. If you maintain this consistency, you'll have engaged in hundreds of discreet business development actions and will have observed the compounding effect of your efforts. It's like fertilizing a massive field from which you will harvest significant revenue for both you and your network. In one of my favorite quotes, Greek philosopher, Epictetus, sums up the importance of consistency and commitment:

> *Tentative efforts lead to tentative outcomes. Therefore, give yourself fully to your endeavors. Decide to construct your character through excellent actions and determine to pay the price of a worthy goal. The trials you encounter will introduce you to your strengths. Remain steadfast...and one day you will build something that endures, something worthy of your potential.*

Persistence and Tenacity

IF YOU LOOK AT successful people in any field, you will not necessarily find the strongest or smartest, but the ones with the most drive, tenacity, and determination. I believe that the formula to successfully achieving anything in life is desire, effective strategy, consistent action, and persistence. Luck also plays an important role, but you can influence the likelihood of being lucky by working hard, following a strategic plan, and seizing opportunities.

By reading this book, you have demonstrated the desire to grow professionally and personally. But do you believe you can accomplish your business development goals? Henry Ford said, "Whether you think you can, or you think you can't—you're right." I believe in the power of confidence and positive thinking; it creates an energy that attracts more positivity. You must believe that you can accomplish the goals you have set, but believing is not enough. It takes consistent action, determination, persistence, and a good strategy. This book provides the strategy to turn your dreams into reality, but it will be of little value if not consistently applied with fierce determination. Calvin Coolidge observed the importance of persistence:

> *Nothing in this world can take the place of persistence. Talent will not; nothing is more common than unsuccessful men with talent. Genius will not; unrewarded genius is almost a proverb. Education will not; the world is full of educated derelicts. Persistence and determination alone are omnipotent.*

So what is persistence? The Oxford Dictionary defines

persistence as follows: "Firm or obstinate continuance in a course of action in spite of difficulty or opposition." Failure, too. I added the last part because, in my experience, constructively addressing failure is critical. Nobody likes failing, being rejected, losing a trial, experiencing a broken deal, facing a displeased client, or countless other manifestations of failure in the context of delivering professional services. But failure is the building block of success. I have learned the hard way that one's attitude toward failure is critical. I try to interpret failure as simply an undesirable outcome, knowing that it is temporary and will teach me how to refine my strategy or do something differently the next time.

This logical analysis is often difficult to summon in the face of a bruised ego. As such, when I fail to achieve a desired outcome, I have to remind myself how commonplace it is among the most successful people in all aspects of life. The greatest baseball hitters of all-time hit just over .350. That means they struck out, or failed, nearly seven times out of ten. Remembering the following notorious examples has helped me put my failure into perspective.

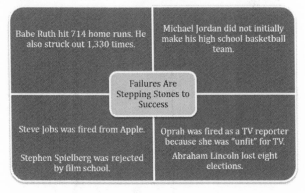

Babe Ruth hit 714 home runs. He also struck out 1,330 times.

Michael Jordan did not initially make his high school basketball team.

Failures Are
Stepping Stones to
Success

Steve Jobs was fired from Apple.

Stephen Spielberg was rejected by film school.

Oprah was fired as a TV reporter because she was "unfit" for TV.

Abraham Lincoln lost eight elections.

These powerful examples usually snap me out of my pity party. I love the following quote by Napoleon Hill because it reminds me that success is right around the corner from failure: "Before success comes in any man's life, he is sure to meet with much temporary defeat and perhaps some failures. When defeat overtakes a man, the easiest and the most logical thing to do is quit. That is exactly what the majority of men do." I do not want to be like the "majority of men," so I do not quit in the face of challenges and obstacles. Neither should you.

I am fortunate to work with some extraordinarily smart people, most of whom have degrees from Ivy League schools. As for me, I attended good, but far from extraordinary, academic institutions. I am confident that I would not win an IQ test at my investment banking firm, but raw natural intelligence is not what has enabled me to succeed at a young age. I have enough intellect to excel at the technical aspects of my job but attribute much of my success to persistence and tenacity, as illustrated by the following examples.

In the most successful transaction of my career, the client initially rejected me. I was interviewed, thought it went well, and was asked to provide an engagement letter. But I never received a response. I tried other angles and contacted other professionals involved. Despite warm introductions from mutual acquaintances, the client's outside counsel was unresponsive to emails and phone calls. With other avenues exhausted, I drove three hours (round trip) to a public court hearing, hoping I could meet the company's management team or their in-house counsel. Neither gave me the time of day.

Soon, thereafter, I learned that the company intended to hire another investment bank. At that point, most normal people would call it quits. My prospective client was a great company, and I knew that my firm and I were best suited to help it. As such, I ignored the rejection and doubled down my efforts. I shifted strategies and imposed upon a friend who wielded some influence with the company's attorney to secure me another opportunity because my experience was better suited for the engagement. A few days later, I obtained another interview with the company and was ultimately hired. I later learned that another advisor working with the company had created some confusion, which almost resulted in the company hiring a different investment bank. If I had not been persistent, I would have never gotten the opportunity to clear up this confusion and earn several million dollars.

I had a similar experience with a venture capitalist. Having co-founded a technology company, I identified a venture capitalist my partner and I thought would be the perfect fit due to his industry expertise. He initially indicated an interest in investing and then changed his mind when he concluded that the team (my co-founder and I) was deficient. Once my fragile ego recovered from the initial sting, I reengaged him, to his surprise, with a different investment thesis and ultimately persuaded him to invest a significant amount of capital. If I would have simply accepted his initial rejection, that company may not have been positioned for success.

These examples of persistence helped me achieve my desired outcome, but there is not enough space to describe all the times I have been unsuccessful. In those instances, after persisting to no avail, I have recently learned to apply another powerful principle—*acceptance*. A couple of years ago, I learned the tremendous power of acceptance in my personal life, applying it to the tragic murder of my father and the untimely loss of my brother and mother. Since it worked well on more consequential personal matters, I correctly assumed it would be a valuable tool in my professional life.

My knee jerk reaction to an unwanted outcome used to be blaming and brooding, two highly unproductive responses. I had to learn that there were instances when I simply could not control outcomes, how other people acted, or what I received. The philosophy of acceptance was difficult for me to grasp because it seemed to inspire a *laissez-faire* approach to life and contradicted my fundamental belief in hard work and persistence. It took me a while to appreciate that they are not mutually exclusive. Acceptance does not mean that one retreats and sits idly by, hoping for things to go his way. I am responsible for developing and implementing thoughtful strategies, treating people with respect, and making a consistent effort, but at the same time I attempt to detach from the desired outcome. This facilitates the acceptance of whatever result is achieved. I have learned that in the absence of acceptance, our already stressful lives as professional service providers can become extremely frustrating.

I recently listened to an interesting TED talk where

the speaker, success expert Richard St. John, indicated that a leading indicator of success is the ability to persist through CRAP: criticism, rejection, assholes, and pressure. That's good advice and cogently describes my experiences throughout my career. But do not rely on my experiences alone. There is a lot of research showing that having a high IQ is only a small component of achieving professional success and wealth. There are other elements that are more important, such as having a strong work ethic, being persistent, being likeable, and having the ability to read people and situations.

The book, *Emotional Intelligence*, by Daniel Goleman states, "Psychologists agree that IQ contributes only about twenty percent of the factors that determine success. A full eighty percent come from other factors, including what I call emotional intelligence." This emotional intelligence exists in all of us. I derived a great deal from my childhood, where I experienced some things you would not expect from a white, clean-cut, Jewish kid. I witnessed a few stabbings, a friend of a friend shot in the face, and a lot of fighting. This forced me to become street-smart, self-reliant, and to develop emotional intelligence.

I encourage you to look inside yourself for challenging experiences that forced you to grow mentally, spiritually, and emotionally. When a potential client rejects you, or an adversary belittles you, remember them and draw strength from these experiences. It will put the encounter in perspective and give you the fortitude to continue pursuing your goals. Forging ahead in the face of obstacles and challenges is what distinguishes "average" from "exceptional."

Grow Existing Clients

When you're fortunate enough to secure your own clients, it's a given that you must provide sound advice. That's expected. If you want to stand out in your client's mind, you need to do the *unexpected*. This is critical to your overall business development strategy because it's far easier to secure more business from an existing client than landing a new one. So…how do you stand out?

In addition to incorporating the branding and likeability strategies discussed earlier, return emails and phone calls immediately. Send emails early in the morning, late at night, and on the weekend to show your clients how committed you are to their matters. Deep relationships are built in person. Make the time to visit your clients in their offices, tour their facilities, and meet other members of their team. Learn the intricacies of your client's business and industry and know the outside forces that may influence its performance. For example, if your client is a healthcare provider, and there is an obscure law going into effect that may change reimbursement procedures that's getting little attention in the media, proactively review it and advise your client of the implications. While this may result in creating an additional assignment for your firm, it should not be your primary agenda. The goal is to show that you understand your client's business and care about its success.

This strategy is most effective if you are both intimately

familiar with your client's business and are consistently consuming relevant knowledge, such as reading local and national newspapers, trade journals, and business magazines. Be proactive about other ways you can add value, like introducing them to a potential client or organizing a substantive workshop for their employees. As you consistently deliver sound advice and unusually good service, your client will begin to trust you, and that is when the magic starts to happen. Once you become a trusted advisor to your client contact, you have the opportunity to influence his or her decisions with regard to hiring other professionals. In turn, you will get opportunities to refer your target referral sources, which will grow your client base exponentially.

Become the Trusted Advisor

EARLIER WE DISCUSSED THE importance of befriending trusted advisors, but becoming one is the holy grail. I cannot sufficiently emphasize the importance of becoming a trusted advisor to clients, target clients, and referral sources, as well as friends, colleagues, family, and your entire professional network. By becoming a trusted advisor, your counsel is immediately sought when an urgent issue arises because you have established yourself as someone who provides shrewd, objective, and insightful advice—a precious commodity with many benefits.

First, it leads to recurring business representations with clients who are less price sensitive. Second, it enables you to avoid the time and energy wasted on creating and shaping impressions at the outset of a relationship. You

can be your authentic self and offer guidance in an efficient, unpackaged manner. Finally, it affords you an unusual amount of influence over various affairs, including
the hiring of service providers—ideally your target referral sources. For example, I recently helped a friend understand his liability as a board member of a failing company.
I knew there was not an opportunity for me to provide
investment banking services because the company was
not salvageable, but I had the expertise to help him spot
issues and develop a strategy for dealing with them. After
investing a number of hours, it became apparent that the
board should hire independent counsel, which I helped
facilitate.

As you transform into a trusted advisor, the influence
you exert on the hiring of target referral sources should
not be taken lightly. You should only refer professionals
whose skills and integrity you have the utmost confidence
in. Equally important is a belief that there will be a good
personality fit. A company we sold a few years ago had
been founded by a humble, blue-collar self-made man.
Someone referred a wealth manager to him. The wealth
manager showed up at the owner's manufacturing plant in
a Bentley, bragging about how much he manages and the
wealth he had amassed. You can surmise that Mr. Flashy
Wealth Manager did not get our client's business. More
importantly, it tainted our client's perspective on the colleague who had referred him.

There are many elements that go into becoming a
trusted advisor, and there is no magic bullet. Trust is built

gradually by consistently engaging in a pattern of ethical behavior that is encapsulated in your personal brand.

- ❯ Demonstrate honesty, integrity, and discretion in all aspects of your life.
- ❯ Respect other people's time and pay attention to them, not your phone.
- ❯ Always be prepared for a meeting and add value.
- ❯ Be generous with your knowledge and offer insightful thoughts, ideas, and strategies.
- ❯ Follow up on any commitments you make, no matter how small. If you tell someone that you will send an email later in the day, make sure you do it.
- ❯ Exhibit a positive attitude and do not be critical or judgmental of others.
- ❯ Empathize and show genuine interest in other people's problems and earnestly attempt to resolve them.
- ❯ Do not exaggerate or lie. If you don't know something, admit it.
- ❯ Give advice that is adverse to your personal interest.

These small things, taken together, create your reputation as someone who can be trusted. These inward trust-building activities can be reinforced by external factors. Your expertise, as evidenced by accolades you've won, articles you've written, quotes in the press, seminars at which you presented, boards on which you sit, also conveys trust.

In order to maximize your opportunities to serve as a

trusted advisor, you need to have a broad base of knowledge. I like to say that I'm a jack-of-all-trades but a master of none. I have diverse experience as a result of being a lawyer, investment banker, and entrepreneur, and I'm constantly pursuing additional knowledge by continuously reading business and self-help books, auditing classes, and studying coursework online.

That said, all the knowledge in the world is of little use if you are not a good listener. You must be extremely inquisitive because the hallmark of a professional service provider is being an effective listener and problem solver. Whether you are speaking with a friend, target referral source, or target client, you should never offer your opinion until you fully understand the nature of the problem and the person's motivation. If there is any confusion as to the former, restate the issue, so the problem can be clearly defined. Oftentimes, people will identify elements of the solution by verbal or non-verbal cues and reveal their desired outcome, and you must include that in your advice. It is akin to incorporating the professor's thoughts into a test answer, which is usually the difference between a B and an A—a concept I failed to fully grasp until my thirties. The reality is that knowing the correct technical answer is not always sufficient.

Being a trusted advisor requires the ability to communicate advice in a way that resonates with clients and influences their decisions. Professional advice is not always evaluated rationally, based on logic and reason. Rather, it is interpreted by individuals through the lens of their collective experiences, objectives, preferences, biases, and emotional state. Two clients in the exact same situation can interpret the same advice very differently. One may view your advice as being practical and shrewd, while the other sees it as misguided and naive. As a result of a complex web of factors that cause each of us to view the same situation differently, being a truly effective advisor requires the perceptive packaging of advice based on your insight into your client's motivation, desired outcome, and emotional state. Knowing the right answer is of limited value if your client is unwilling to accept it, so you must not only understand the problem but also how to effectively present the solution.

There are times when I get frustrated with clients as they procrastinate and struggle with the solution that seems so clear to me. In those instances, I must remember that while I have ridden this bull a hundred times before, this is their first rodeo. I try to be patient, resist the temptation to lecture, and remind myself that my clients are humans not machines processing data. A trusted advisor is emotionally connected to his or her client and instinctively knows when to shift from advisor to confidant, psychologist, or friend. I then try to engage them in a collaborative dialogue, where we review the pros and cons of various strategies and attempt to lead my client to developing the most suitable solution. At times, this process can be painful and feel like a bad flashback to the Socratic Method employed by my professors during law school. However, if done successfully, this process of consensus building leads to clients feeling empowered and developing greater trust.

CHAPTER 4

Meditation – The X Factor

The biggest barrier to becoming a rainmaker and trusted advisor, and building a life and career beyond our dreams, is us.

While I lack any scientific credentials, my experience as a human tells me it's our nature to be self-centered. It probably stems from our primitive programming and survival instincts, but the root cause is not important. What is essential to appreciate is that it's hard to be an effective advisor and problem solver while constantly distracted by our natural instinct to focus on our own interests, wants, and desires. Only by being present can we truly focus on, and empathize with, someone else's problems, establish trust, and build powerful bonds. To do so, we must become consciously aware of our egos in action.

We are all bombarded by thousands of thoughts each day—fears, insecurities, resentments, and a range of other unproductive emotions that are manifestations of our egos. Each of us has a voice in our head that produces incessant, judgmental chatter that interferes with our productivity and serenity. And the advertising industry has done a terrific job appealing to our insatiable egos, persuading us that once we get the shiny car, new house, expensive watch, fabulous wardrobe, or whatever else, we will be content and happy. Likewise, we think once we become partners, managing directors, or achieve some other professional accomplishment, we will be content.

It is not true!

I have come to learn that except in cases of actual poverty, there is a low correlation between material wealth and happiness. As I've experienced, our egos are never fully satisfied because our material and career goals are moving targets. We are only briefly satisfied when a specific goal, want, or desire is achieved. We quickly become accustomed to our newest accomplishments and the habitual process of yearning starts all over again. Objectively speaking, most of us have everything we need to be happy—food, shelter, employment, our senses, intellect, friends, family, and other positive attributes and resources. The question then is how do we quiet our minds' incessant chatter, which distracts us from achieving our true potential?

The answer is meditation.

Meditation is an extraordinarily effective tool to help you achieve your potential by quieting the inner voice that judges you, tells you that you are not good enough or do not have enough, forces you to live in the painful memories of the past or projections of the future, and provokes conflicts with friends, family, and colleagues. Meditation helps us gain awareness of our obsessive thoughts and build concentration, which enables us to be more present, serene, and productive. Have you ever been in a meeting with a more senior colleague or client and become insecure about your knowledge of the topic being discussed or your performance? If so, you can probably appreciate how this fleeting thought can quickly poison your consciousness and blossom into a compelling and obsessive distraction. Within seconds, you are no longer focused on your interaction. Rather, you are obsessing about how you are being perceived and the potential consequences of that perception on your career and life.

Another example to which you may relate is the need to be right. It is Ego 101 to be right, to prove your point and demonstrate superiority. This phenomenon is magnified in the professional services industry as we spend ten hours a day relying on our intellect to provide advice that we expect to be followed. When our advice is not followed or our perspective is challenged, our egos are severely threatened. Once our egos start driving the bus, we often lose all perspective and are compelled to defend it at all costs. Our ability to use logic and reason is hijacked by emotions and the ego's extraordinary need to be victorious. This is highly unproductive and an impediment to achieving business objectives, serenity, and happiness.

I have found that consistently practicing meditation results in a newfound awareness, a pause button of sorts. It enables you to carefully assess situations that may engender conflict to determine whether it is truly important to be right (such as in a business negotiation where a deal term is inaccurately memorialized in an agreement), or whether the urge to engage is purely ego-based. Resisting the lure of your ego can be challenging, but you will be amazed by the liberation that comes with relinquishing the need to constantly persuade others with your point of view.

Lest you think that I've traded in my capitalist ideology for some new-age nonsense, I am not suggesting that it is inappropriate to be ambitious, successful, or acquire nice things. Indeed, this book is designed to help you achieve financial success, so that you can more fully enjoy life. But it would be incomplete if I did not extol the power of meditation, as it has dramatically improved my professional (and personal) life. Fortunately, you do not have to take my word for it; there's a plethora of successful people from all walks of life who rely on daily meditation to improve their professional and personal lives. The world's leading academic institutions, including Harvard, Yale, and the University of Pennsylvania, have scientifically validated the tremendous benefits of meditation. For example, in 2012, the *Harvard Business Review* published an article stating, "Meditation brings many benefits: It refreshes us, helps us settle into what's happening now, makes us wiser and gentler, helps us cope in a world that overloads us with information and communication, and more." It makes us more productive by "increasing…[our] capacity to resist distracting urges" by strengthening our "willpower muscle."

Leading neuroscientists have recently concluded that meditation permanently strengthens, changes, and improves our brain function. It improves our mood, cognitive functioning, and outlook on life. Hedy Kober, professor of psychology at Yale University, and Director of Research at the Yale Therapeutic Neuroscience Clinic, explains the amazing power of meditation in profoundly simple terms: "Shit happens," which is the bad news, but the good news is through meditation "each and every one of you has the power to control and change your experience of this shit when it happens…feel less stressed, less pain, improve cognitive functions and overall wellbeing, and change how your brain works."

I have found meditation to be both simple and incredibly challenging. In a nutshell, it is simply the concentrated focus on your breath. When a thought or other distraction enters your mind, you simply refocus on your breath. When I first started meditating, I thought I was failing because I could not stop my thoughts from polluting my consciousness. It took me a while to realize that this is normal. Proficiency in meditation involves the quick non-judgmental identification of thoughts and equally quick ability to refocus on your breath. If you have never meditated, I'm sure it sounds ridiculous that focusing on your breath for twenty minutes a day can dramatically improve your life. But this simple practice teaches a newfound awareness of our thoughts and emotions and reveals how not to attach to them, which can be highly distracting, unproductive, and potentially destructive. It creates space, a brief pause, between stimulus and response. This is incredibly important for us as professional service providers because we are constantly antagonized by clients and opposing adversaries and beset by internal and external pressures we place on ourselves.

I have come to appreciate that meditation, like business development efforts, needs to be practiced daily. Think of it like mental exercise. You will not see results overnight, but pretty soon you will appreciate how meditation will make you less reactive to situations such as a client or a partner mistreating you. It will make you more aware of your thoughts as they occur, which will help you pause before turning a fleeting thought into an anxiety producing drama.

Meditation will also make you less reliant on external stimuli and circumstances for your happiness. The little conflicts, ruminations about the past, and worry of the future that saps your mental and emotional energy will be noticeably lessened. You will experience an unusual calm and focus, which will improve all aspects of your personal and professional life.

There are a myriad of great books on the purpose and practice of meditation and attendant Eastern philosophy. Four of my favorites that I frequently recommend are:

> ❯ *Search Inside Yourself: The Unexpected Path to Achieving Success, Happiness (and World Peace)* by Google engineer Chade-Meng Tan
> ❯ *The Power of Now: A Guide to Spiritual Enlightenment* by Eckhart Tolle
> ❯ *Real Happiness: The Power of Meditation* by Sharon Salzberg
> ❯ *Happiness: A Guide to Developing Life's Most Important Skill* by Matthieu Ricard

CHAPTER 5

Start Your Journey

As we conclude our journey together, you now have tools at your disposal to become a rainmaker and improve the quality of your life. I hope I helped you to rethink some of your preconceived notions and inspired you to continue on your own journey of professional and personal self-transformation. I'm confident that the strategies articulated in this book will help you become a rainmaker because they are based not on theory or conjecture, but experience. I did not invent these techniques; I have simply taken what I've learned from mentors, books, seminars, and a lot of trial and error and synthesized the concepts into a replicable and easy-to-follow six-step formula:

1. Set Goals
2. Build Your Brand
3. Accelerate Growth
4. Define and Build Your Network
5. Work Your Network
6. Find a Mentor

If you consistently follow this formula, incorporate my success strategies, and practice meditation, you will earn considerably more money and have more freedom, but that is not all. By adhering to the underlying theme of this book of genuinely helping others succeed, you will experience a greater level of happiness and meaning. It's the ultimate win-win strategy.

Helping others achieve success and happiness in their lives is so powerful because it distracts our natural inclination to be self-centered, which is usually the culprit of most of our stress, anger, frustration, and resentments, and is an impediment to becoming an effective advisor and rainmaker.

Conclusion

THANK YOU FOR READING *Rain Power*. I invite you to start helping yourself and others succeed in all aspects of their lives by joining a community of like-minded individuals (search for the group entitled *Rain Power* on LinkedIn). Remember, only by helping others achieve their goals can you truly succeed in business and in life.